T0319064

Cambridge Elements ≡

Elements in Public and Nonprofit Administration
edited by
Andrew Whitford
University of Georgia
Robert Christensen
Brigham Young University

RACE, POLICING, AND PUBLIC GOVERNANCE

On the Other Side of Now

Brian N. Williams
University of Virginia
Carmen J. Williams
University of Virginia
Domenick E. Bailey
University of Virginia
Lana Homola
University of Virginia

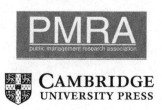

CAMBRIDGE
UNIVERSITY PRESS

CAMBRIDGE
UNIVERSITY PRESS

University Printing House, Cambridge CB2 8BS, United Kingdom

One Liberty Plaza, 20th Floor, New York, NY 10006, USA

477 Williamstown Road, Port Melbourne, VIC 3207, Australia

314–321, 3rd Floor, Plot 3, Splendor Forum, Jasola District Centre, New Delhi – 110025, India

79 Anson Road, #06–04/06, Singapore 079906

Cambridge University Press is part of the University of Cambridge.

It furthers the University's mission by disseminating knowledge in the pursuit of education, learning, and research at the highest international levels of excellence.

www.cambridge.org
Information on this title: www.cambridge.org/9781108972857
DOI: 10.1017/9781108973199

© Brian N. Williams, Carmen J. Williams, Domenick E. Bailey, and Lana Homola 2021

This publication is in copyright. Subject to statutory exception and to the provisions of relevant collective licensing agreements, no reproduction of any part may take place without the written permission of Cambridge University Press.

First published 2021

A catalogue record for this publication is available from the British Library.

ISBN 978-1-108-97285-7 Paperback
ISSN 2515-4303 (online)
ISSN 2515-429X (print)

Cambridge University Press has no responsibility for the persistence or accuracy of URLs for external or third-party internet websites referred to in this publication and does not guarantee that any content on such websites is, or will remain, accurate or appropriate.

Race, Policing, and Public Governance

On the Other Side of Now

Elements in Public and Nonprofit Administration

DOI: 10.1017/9781108973199
First published online: June 2021

Brian N. Williams
University of Virginia

Carmen J. Williams
University of Virginia

Domenick E. Bailey
University of Virginia

Lana Homola
University of Virginia

Author for correspondence: Brian N. Williams, Bnw9q@virginia.edu

Abstract: *I can't breathe* ... a haunting phrase moaned at the intersection of past and present, serving as an audible supplement to the visual evidence to yet another collision of race and policing. This phrase reflects the current state of police-community relations in the United States. But, what lies on the other side of now? This Element examines this salient question in the context of excessive use of force and through the lenses of race, policing, and public governance. We draw upon extant research and scholarship on representative bureaucracy, public engagement in the cocreation of public polices and the coproduction of public services, and the emerging findings from studies in network science, coupled with insights from elite interviews, to offer implications for future research, the profession of policing, the public policy-making process, public management, and postsecondary institutions.

Keywords: police, systemic racism, public governance, cocreation/ coproduction, use of force

© Brian N. Williams, Carmen J. Williams, Domenick E. Bailey, and Lana Homola 2021

ISBNs: 9781108972857 (PB), 9781108973199 (OC)
ISSNs: 2515-4303 (online), 2515-429X (print)

Contents

1 Introduction

"On the Other Side of Now" . . . by Brian N. Williams

I am perplexed . . . What happens on the other side of now?
What lessons will we learn?
What reforms will be considered and discussed?
Who will be involved in this process? What will their level of involvement be? Who will decide?
What resources will be suggested? Recommended? Appropriated? Allocated? Used?
Where will those resources come from?
How will police policies, procedures and practices change?

In spite of my perplexity, I am hopeful . . . .
When I recall the images of the beautiful and heart lifting mosaic of black, white, brown, he, she, we, they, trans, straight, gay, bi, queer, single, married, divorced, partner, Christian, Muslim, Jewish, Sikh, Hindu, Buddhist, agnostic, atheist, questioning, rural, suburban, urban, local, national, continental, global marching and protesting mass of shared humanity.

Yet, in the face of my hope, I am concerned . . .
When this news cycle ends, how long will we remember?
If another incident occurs, what happens then?
How much more disappointment and pain can we take?
How much longer can dreams be deferred and justice be denied?
What happens after the events of then?

Regardless of my concerns, I am resolute . . .
I must and we must embrace, lean in to, and act because of the urgency of now!

1.1 The Backdrop

The ultimate measure of a man is not where he stands in moments of comfort and convenience, but where he stands at times of challenge and controversy.
– Martin Luther King, Jr.

We are living in a time of challenge and controversy – not one of comfort and convenience. The events of 2020 reflect the emergence and reemergence of wicked problems (Head, 2008) that impact public policy and professional practices. These problems are invisible, yet visible, perplexing and pernicious, complex and intractable. The convergence and coupling of past and present viruses, racism, and COVID-19 crises have created what some describe as a pandemic within a pandemic.[1] Both viruses are highly contagious, imperceptible, hidden,

---

[1] Sheryl Gay Stolberg, 2020. "Pandemic within a pandemic": Coronavirus and police brutality roil black communities." *The New York Times.*

and deadly. Vaccines have not been developed to prevent or cure them, but strategies are emerging that limit their effects. One advocates social distancing as a mitigating approach; the other requires social engagement as a moderating stratagem, where more meaningful interactions can lead to deeper understanding and appreciation for the other. We are at a nexus, stopped at the intersection of past and present. Trying to gather our wits, still our hearts, minds, and bodies. We are troubled and tired, anguished and anxious, worried about what is on the other side of now.

We have arrived at a defining moment (Badaracco, 1997) in time. We are at a time for much-needed inquiry and analysis, a time of oppositional debate and collaborative dialogue. We are at a time of discovery and revelation; a time that exposes who we are and what we value. We have arrived at a time that requires introspection – at the individual, organizational, institutional, societal, and global level.

Much like the seminal work of Dickens (2007), we are at the best and worst of times, trying to make our way during this age of wisdom and foolishness; belief and incredulity; of Light and darkness; of hope and despair. We are at a time of technical rationality. Yet, at these crossroads, we have an opportunity to be recalled to life.

Our legacy on the other side of now has yet to be determined. We are still musing which path to take. Going back won't work – because that is a path where the past will serve as prologue. Do we turn left, right, or go blindly ahead? Or, do we critically evaluate the historic harms of our past, appreciate how those have impacted our present, and then chart a new course in our navigational devices and blaze a new trail?

This Element inspires policy makers, public and nonprofit administrators, students of public affairs, and members of the mass, general, and attentive publics to embrace and lean in to this opportunity to contemplate, interrogate, discuss, and decide where do we go from here. We can be proactive in a coactive way. We don't have to be reactive – an ounce of prevention is better than a pound of cure. With the cocreation of just and equitable, intentional and meaningful public policies, supported by professionals and members of the public who are compassionate actors who codesign policies, programs, and services, we can coproduce efforts that lead to better communities. There can be a brighter future on the other side of now. But it depends upon us.

1.2 The Mattering of Lives?

What happens to a dream deferred? What happens when justice is denied? What inner-city blues[2] emerge? Does it make you wanna holler?

---

[2] Marvin Gaye, 1971. "Inner City Blues (Make Me Wanna Holler)."

What happens when deaths of unarmed black and brown men like George Floyd, Sean Monterrosa, Eric Garner, and others occur while in police custody? What happens when black citizens like Botham Jean, Breonna Taylor, and Atatiana Jefferson are shot and killed by police inside their own residences?

What happens when black and brown men who are in their cars, like Mike Ramos, Philando Castille, Erik Salgado, and Samuel DuBose, are fatally shot during a nonthreatening traffic stop? What happens when black boys like Tamir Rice, Antwon Rose, and Laquan McDonald lose their lives from encounters with police? What happens when the world watches the intentional actions of homicidal officers – the firing of eight fatal shots at Walter Scott or the casual kneeling on the neck of a "suspect" by an officer and the subsequent inactions of three others that lead to the death of a man?

What happens to public trust and confidence in the profession of policing and in the criminal justice system? What happens to the morale of officers? What happens to the social fabric of America?

What happens when we see lives in black, brown, white, and blue? Do the lives of those who are white and black in blue matter more than the lives of those who are black or brown? What's going on?[3]

During 2020, we witnessed what happened when peoples' hopes and wishes waxed and waned. Out of the despair and darkness of that moment, a ray of light appeared. The lives of the socially constructed, historically marginalized, oppressed, and criminalized seem to finally matter after protests propelled discussions to modify police policies and practices.[4] Change is in the air and some change – like reallocating police resources in New York City, engaging with members of the public to reimagine and reorganize some police departments, and dismantling the Minneapolis Police Department – has occurred within the profession of policing. But will these and related efforts be enough? Will they be replicated and sustained across law enforcement agencies? After the urgency of the present, what will happen when the media attention is no longer there? Will the black and brown lives that are not in blue matter on the other side of now?

1.3 Excessive Use of Force: A Wicked Problem and Its Environment

Police departments are essential in supporting the American concept of democracy. They have been tasked with protecting life, liberty, and property, and in order to carry out their official duties, police have a monopoly on enacting the state's

---

[3] Marvin Gaye, 1971. "What's Going On."

[4] Lindsey Van Ness, 2020. Protests prompt policing changes, but skeptics doubt they will be enough. *PEW Charitable Trusts.*

legitimate use of force (Weber, 1994). Police officers, as street-level bureaucrats, have discretion in carrying out their responsibilities, which create individual dilemmas that can impact a department and a profession (Lipsky, 2010).

Use of force is associated with the amount of effort required by police to induce compliance by an unwilling person. This concept is linked to a continuum that includes basic verbal commands, physical restraint, less-than-lethal force, and lethal force. It is commonly agreed upon that police officers should limit the use of physical force to that which is necessary to mitigate an incident, make an arrest, or protect themselves or others from harm (Alpert & Dunham, 2004). In essence, use of force is an officer's last option to restore safety within a community when other measures fail. Yet, the level of force that an officer uses will vary due to the situation and his or her discretion. The discretion used by officers has been shown to be deadly in some encounters and highlight the failure of police use of force policies (University of Chicago Law School – Global Human Rights Clinic, 2020).

This Element centers on excessive use of force in the context of racialized policing. Even though there is no universally agreed upon definition of use of force, this concept has been critiqued for lacking basic protections for segments of the public against police violence. Shortcomings have been identified that include:

- Failing to require officers to deescalate situations;
- Failing to require officers to intervene and stop excessive force;
- Failing to restrict officers from shooting at moving vehicles;
- Failing to develop a force continuum that limits the types of weapons and force used to respond to specific types of resistance;
- Failing to request officers to give verbal warning and exhausting other reasonable means prior to resorting to deadly force;
- Failing to require that officers report each time they threaten or use excessive force; and
- Permitting officers to choke or strangle civilians.

These failures jeopardize the standing of the police as guarantors of bedrock values of American society, like promoting domestic tranquility and assuring justice that are embedded within the Preamble of the US Constitution and highlight the challenging, and in some respects, impossible job that police departments and officers have (Morrell & Currie, 2015).

Police departments operate in the midst of a socially complex, wicked problem environment (Conklin, 2006). They are expected to address complicated and thorny issues but are challenged by lack of information, an incomplete understanding of the problem and its related symptoms, limited resources, and differing and conflicting perspectives of stakeholders with no commonly agreed-upon strategy to mitigate this issue. As public organizations, police departments operate within an open system, impacted by a web of politics, and face challenges associated with polycentricity (Grandage, Aliperti & Williams, 2018). They produce outputs like number of contacts with citizens or residents, citations written, arrests made, and cases solved that are easily quantifiable and might resonate with certain segments of the public but, in many respects, are controversial to other segments. These outputs impact public perception for the worse, especially along the American color spectrum – from black to white. Public opinion polls show that in light of recent events, favorable opinions of the police have significantly decreased across all races. Results from the Democracy Fund + UCLA Nationscape Project survey show a decrease in favorability from 47 to 38 percent of black respondents and 72 to 61 percent of white respondents (Morin, 2020). Similarly, results from the ABC News and Ipsos poll indicate people are also realizing that these events are not isolated incidents: 74 percent of respondents now agree that the deaths of George Floyd and others are representative of a greater issue (Jackson & Newall, 2020).[5]

Police departments also produce outcomes that are much more difficult to measure. These outcomes are very visible and can produce a visceral reaction. The deaths of George Floyd, Breonna Taylor, and others are dystopian outcomes that have led to global protests. Contemporary reactions may be the result of a gradual and growing outrage. Protests may be in response to the fear that America's past is prologue, considering that police interactions with black and brown people seem to perpetuate and propel the historical narrative that black and brown bodies, like black and brown lives, still don't matter. This disheartening suspicion has had a crescendo effect – that justice delayed is justice denied.

1.4 The Search for Justice as a Sisyphean Task

The current state of police-community relations is precarious due to a growing demand that America lives up to its ideals – that black and brown Americans are valued too. It's been nearly sixty years since Dr. Martin Luther King, Jr.'s famous speech in Washington. Yet, his poignant words ring true today.

> In a sense, we have come to our nation's capital to cash a check. When the architects of our republic wrote the magnificent words of the Constitution and

---

[5] Chris Jackson and Mallor Newall, 2020. Americans overwhelmingly view Floyd killing as part of larger problem. *ABC News*/Ipsos.

the Declaration of Independence, they were signing a promissory note to which every American was to fall heir.

This note was a promise that all men, yes, black men as well as white men, would be guaranteed the inalienable rights of life, liberty, and the pursuit of happiness.

It is obvious today that America has defaulted on this promissory note insofar as her citizens of color are concerned. Instead of honoring this sacred obligation, America has given the Negro people a bad check, a check which has come back marked "insufficient funds." But we refuse to believe that the bank of justice is bankrupt. We refuse to believe that there are insufficient funds in the great vaults of opportunity of this nation. So, we have come to cash this check – a check that will give us upon demand the riches of freedom and the security of justice.

Black and brown people are still waiting to cash their check. Funds are still insufficient. Deaths from benign encounters cannot be explained. Consequently, the search for justice and its security remains to many, a Sisyphean task.

Much like the Greek mythical figure King Sisyphus, people of color seem to be punished perpetually – forever rolling a boulder up a hill from the depths of Hades. Whenever it seems that progress is being made – after the death of America's first patriot and freedom fighter Crispus Attucks, after the war over slavery, after valiantly serving in the great world wars, after the civil rights movement, after the election of the first black president – the boulder rolls back into the depths of the hellish place that some see America as continuing to be. The cycle is repeated. There seems to be a symmetry or consistency between the experiences of America's past and its present. But unlike King Sisyphus, who twice cheated death and was infamous for his chicanery, the punishment exacted upon black and brown people is undeserved and, in some instances of encounters with police, is life ending.

1.5 At the Intersection of Past and Present

The haunting, painstaking plea of "I can't breathe"[6] reverberates – from Eric Garner in Staten Island, New York, to George Floyd in Minneapolis, Minnesota, to Manuel Ellis in Tacoma, Washington. It attunes the ears and fixes the eyes on the problem of excessive and, in these instances, deadly use of force by those sworn to serve and protect.

"I can't breathe" echoes and now brings to the forefront of a global consciousness audible and visual evidence from the not-so-distant past and even in the present. Bygone voices have expressed similar sentiments but were not believed. Expressions akin to "I can't breathe" like "I can't live where I would

---

[6] H.E.R, 2020. "I Can't Breathe."

like to live," "I can't go to school where I would like to go to school," "I can't get the job that aligns with my credentials," or "I can't get the wages that are due me because of my skin color or gender" have gone unheard from the invisible, minoritized, marginalized, and dehumanized commodities before the rebellion for slavery and beyond.

"I can't breathe . . . " yet echoes in the land of utopia – the focal location of democracy and its theoretical values of individual rights, the pursuit of happiness, and justice for all. America. Its exceptionalism and emphasis on meritocracy. America. The place where unpaid and underpaid labor[7] has had a transgenerational impact on black people in particular. America. The focal location and laboratory for the great social experiment. In this place of utopian declarations, the dystopian cry of "I can't breathe . . . " continues. A cascading cacophony flowing from the American past to the American present. Unmelodious. Discordant. Noise. White noise. Silence. In the land of the free[8] yet another black man is in the bag and another stain is on its flag.

This plaintiff cry for help, for assistance, for recognition of humanity to other humans has been rebuffed, rejected, unheard, disregarded – disgustingly so by some elected and appointed public servants, by politicians, and by professionals across the criminal justice system. This seems to be the case when wails come from minoritized, marginalized, and historically harmed populations like members of the African American community. The unresponsiveness from some of those who have sworn an oath and embraced a code to protect and serve is most disheartening. Those directly involved and others in their complicity have rejected the principles of democratic policing as articulated by Sir Robert Peel.

But others have heard the plaintive cries for help. Like the lyrics of one of Bob Marley's songs of protest, people are getting up and standing up for their rights.[9] The cries arise from the protests of locals in cities, towns, and hamlets large and small across the United States to the gatherings of globals in countries and time zones that span the spaces and places of this earth that we share. American society is now resting at the intersection of the preceding and the existent. At this intersection choices will have to be made: Evolution or revolution? Reform or riots? To defund and divest or to deconstruct and reconstruct? Where do we go from here? Will a phoenix arise from these ashes? Will peace be found, stilled, and settled out of this storm? No more water . . . will there be more fire the next time?[10] Out of this darkness, will light appear? What happens on the other side of now?

---

[7] Danyelle Solomon, Connor Maxwell, and Abril Castro, 2019. Systemic inequality and economic opportunity. *Center for American Progress.*

[8] The Killers, 2020. "Land of the Free."   [9] Bob Marley, 1973. "Get Up, Stand Up."

[10] James Baldwin, 1963. "The Fire Next Time (read by Jesse L. Martin)."

1.6 Goal, Resulting Approach, and Distinctiveness of Element

Race, Policing, and Public Governance: On the Other Side of Now will answer these questions by drawing upon

- the theoretical underpinnings of representative bureaucracy, network science, and cocreation and coproduction of public value;
- an approach that examines the past to understand the present and plan for the future;
- a review and unpacking of case law related to police use of force; and
- the wisdom of formal and informal community leaders, secondary and post-secondary students, and police practitioners and executives.

It offers directions and shares a pathway that can have a positive impact on relational policing efforts on the other side of now. The Element examines the past to understand the present-day impact on race, policing, and public governance. It is designed for use in the classroom, training academy, and the community to help students with a passion for public affairs, to encourage community residents involved in advocacy and action, and to motivate policy makers and police practitioners to engage collaboratively with others in understanding and addressing the problem of excessive use of force and reimagining policing. Our intent is to speak across audiences and cultures: the young, the old, the in between; those whose humanities come in shades of black, brown, and white; those who reside at the local, regional, national, continental, and global levels.

Our approach to this Element is unique. It provides an opportunity for us to model what we research and what I as a professor teach and preach: the importance of coupling members of the public with the police in reimagining and redesigning public safety, in cocreating and coproducing community well-being. Our Element takes a similar approach. It identifies, assembles, marshals, and manages needed resources, including persons from different backgrounds and experiences to assist in recognizing and acknowledging the problem and managing with sensitivity the process to develop a plan of action that mitigates that problem.

Our approach to coauthorship – coupling students at the University of Virginia with a relatively more senior researcher and scholar in problem identification, problem understanding, and mitigation – serves as a model. Our method demonstrates what we value and practice: diversity, equity, and inclusion. It encourages and actualizes the facilitation and resulting impact of a collaborative approach to knowledge, intellectual power, and freedom to act upon a shared sense of knowledge and intellectual power.

So, what lies ahead? In Section 2, we highlight the theoretical connections that guide our efforts. Attention is devoted to representative bureaucracy, network science, and cocreation and coproduction. A review of what takes place at the interplay of race, policing, and public governance will then ensue. This will allow for an examination of the past and how that past has a presence in the present while providing an opportunity for a discussion of future prescriptions.

The Element then segues into exploring the implications for the future. Special emphasis is placed on the profession of policing, new directions for research, the public policy-making process in the context of police reform, the governance challenge facing public management and, for pedagogical processes, to better prepare prepublic and nonprofit students in postsecondary institutions. We conclude the Element with a clarion call to action, followed by an epilogue, and finally an appendix with teaching aids for instruction that lists songs of "progress," a link to a perspective-taking video, and links to all of the YouTube videos that we have embedded in this Element.

2 Theoretical Connections

We draw upon three strands of scholarship to explore race, policing, and public governance on the other side of now. Those strands are connected to representative bureaucracy, cocreation and coproduction, and network science. Each will be described in the subsequent paragraphs.

2.1 Representative Bureaucracy

The theory of representative bureaucracy concerns how the demographic characteristics of bureaucrats affect the distribution of services to clients who share these same demographic characteristics. For representative bureaucracy to affect an organization, agents of the organization must be able to act with discretion (Schuck, 2018; Baumgartner et al., 2021). Substantial research has been done on the effects of representation in bureaucracy. Many studies focus specifically on the racial profiling of black citizens and the black community's relationships with law enforcement (Wilkins & Williams, 2008; Nicholson-Crotty et al., 2017; Riccucci et al., 2018; Baumgartner et al., 2021). This area of research is especially relevant to the topic of this Element and salient to the ongoing Black Lives Matter movement.

One important characteristic of representative bureaucracy is the difference between kinds of representation. Extant literature distinguishes between two categories of representation: passive and active. Passive representation focuses on whether the bureaucracy mirrors the demographic dynamics – sex, race, class, religion – as the population it serves (Mosher, 1982). Active representation is concerned with how representation influences policy making and implementation in terms of the delivery of services (Pitkin, 1967).

Previous research probed the link between passive representation and active representation, specifically how passive representation is translated into active representation (Wilkins & Williams, 2008, 2009; Riccucci et al., 2014; Nicholson-Crotty et al., 2017; Schuck, 2018). Others discussed symbolic representation in terms of how representation affects citizens' judgements of law enforcement actions (Riccucci et al., 2018). All three forms of representation are important to consider when understanding the necessity of representative bureaucracy. However, Wilkins & Williams (2008, 2009) and Nicholson-Crotty et al. (2017) found that organizational socialization can override racial ties and block the transition from passive to active representation, therefore not improving (and potentially worsening) racial profiling through increased representation. Organizational socialization is especially apparent in law enforcement agencies such as police departments, demonstrating that demographic representation is not a panacea for all problems and instead must be understood through its greater context.

Representative bureaucracy is often studied in relation to race (Wilkins & Williams, 2008, 2009; Riccucci et al., 2018; Baumgartner et al., 2021; & Nicholson-Crotty et al., 2017) and gender (Riccucci et al., 2014; Schuck, 2018). Although some studies find that having more diverse police officers decreases the prevalence of racial profiling (Riccucci et al., 2018; Baumgartner et al., 2021), others have found that an increase in representation has little effect (Nicholson-Crotty et al., 2017) or even that it actually increases racial profiling (Wilkins & Williams, 2008, 2009). This disparity in results shows that there are other factors that affect racial profiling and that representative bureaucracy is a complex issue, which deserves more investigation.

Another common topic is the representation of women in police divisions, specifically when related to domestic violence and sexual assault cases (Riccucci et al., 2014; Schuck, 2018). Unlike the mixed results from studies on race and representative bureaucracy, studies on gender representation seem to be more conclusive. Both studies found that an increase in the percentage of female police officers in domestic violence units or on sexual assault cases increased the likelihood of women to report cases of sexual assault or domestic violence and increased the likelihood for sexual assault and domestic violence cases to be cleared. Therefore, increasing female representation led to more reporting and more successful cases (Riccucci et al., 2014; Schuck, 2018).

Future research is needed to fill in the gaps of what we know. This knowledge can have a positive impact on policy, programs, and practices that impact people, in general, and black and brown men and women, in particular. Table 1 serves as a summary table highlighting a select group of authors and their findings.

2.2 Network Science: The Social Networks of Police Officers

The heinous murder of George Floyd on May 25, 2020, shocked the world for many reasons, one of which being the number of officers present during the encounter who could have stepped in to prevent Mr. Floyd's death but chose not to. The cruel and unnecessary loss of Floyd's life could not simply be summed up as the actions of one "bad apple," being that there were three other officers on the scene during the eight-minute and forty-six-second ordeal. With the number of officers present, a logical questions arises: Why did none of the other officers do anything to stop former officer Derek Chauvin and save George Floyd? Exploring questions like this requires analyzing the apple and the barrel – the individual officer and the organization. However, a key area of

Table 1 Representative bureaucracy summary

Authors	Findings
Schuck, 2018	– Female representation in sexual assault units increases assault and rape reporting, and victims are more satisfied with their assistance.
Baumgartner et al., 2021	– The most effective police force is one that represents its community with lower rates of searches and more accuracy.
Nicholson-Crotty et al., 2017	– There must be over a critical percent of black officers in a police department for representation to be positive.
Riccucci et al., 2014	– Symbolic representation of gender influences how people perceive law enforcement agencies.
Riccucci et al., 2018	– All racial groups report higher satisfaction with law enforcement agencies that represent them.
Wilkins & Williams, 2008	– Organizational socialization in police culture strips individual goals and replaces them with the organization's goals.
Wilkins & Williams, 2009	– Organizational ties can be stronger than racial ties.

analysis exists between these two levels: the social network within the department.

Network science is an emerging area of research that is uniquely situated between individual and structural levels of analyses (Wood, Roithmayr & Papachristos, 2019). It has been used to study police misconduct, and its findings can identify possible solutions that predict, correct, and prevent misconduct. Network science is a highly interdisciplinary field of research aimed at developing theoretical and practical techniques to increase our understanding of naturally occurring, human-made networks (Börner, Sanyal & Vespignani, 2007). It explores networks in nature, technology, and a wide variety of social spheres. Studies within the past decade have laid the foundation to examine how social networks, and specifically a person's placement within them, can impact outcomes including those related to criminality and delinquency (Papachristos, 2011). Recently network science has been explicitly expanded to the study of police networks, and these studies are now more pertinent than ever.

Deviance exists outside of police communities in ways that are applicable to police communities. Network science has been used to identify the factors that influence the spread of deviant behaviors beyond law enforcement. Examining these studies can yield inferences for how police officers are influenced to behave. A study examining violence in New York City via homicides noted that violent behavior can be effectively passed person-to-person simply through some form of contact or interaction (Fagan, Wilkinson & Davies, 2007). An analogous study looking at social networks' ability to explain and predict gunshot violence in Chicago pointed out that models that incorporated both social contagion and demographic information better predicted gunshot subjects than models that used either of these factors independently (Green, Horel & Papachristos, 2017).

Unlike other areas of life where peer influence and social networks similarly have the power to increase either chances of deviant behavior or conformity to law-abiding behavior, in policing this frequently results in matters of life and death. Studies looking at social contagion and the power of social networks outside of policing would seem to extrapolate to the hypothesis that police, as humans, are not above these same influences when in uniform. It turns out that this hypothesis is correct. It is often the case that the most powerful socialization that humans encounter occurs not in formal network settings but informal ones. Research has shown that it is primarily through the interactions occurring in informal network settings that police are most strongly socialized into their roles as officers (Roithmayr, 2016). Consequently, this socialization has strong effects on perceptions of what constitutes misconduct and deviant behavior (Savitz, 1970). The strength of this influence is demonstrated by field training officers (FTOs), where it was found that about one-quarter of the variation in new police officers' allegations of misconduct were attributable to FTOs (Getty, Worrall & Morris, 2016). Other recent studies into the power of these informal social networks have shown that these findings of simple misconduct can be extended to use of force as well (Ouellet et al., 2019; Quispe-Torreblanca & Stewart, 2019).

One of the most recent studies looking at police networks and use of force has shown that within police social networks, officers who shoot are often characterized as being "brokers" (Zhao & Papachristos, 2020). A broker is like a bridge: an officer who occupies an important intersection that connects other officers who would otherwise not interact with one another due to being in detached parts of the organization. This notion of brokerage also coincides with the concept of betweenness centrality, which is defined as a person having more people linked through them as the shortest path between two people than any other point in the network. Research has found that officers who shoot are higher in betweenness centrality than those who do not (Zhao & Papachristos, 2020).

Network science has yet to establish the direction of the relationship between high activity and high betweenness centrality. In other words, it is not yet clear whether activity facilitates an officer becoming a broker or vice versa. Another important concept known as shuffling – the probability that two randomly selected assignments on which an officer received a complaint are within different units – also exhibits high correlation with brokerage and risk of shooting (Zhao & Papachristos, 2020). What's left to ascertain is how "broker" officers enter into social networks and become these crucial points of contact. It will be important to determine whether brokers are officers that are produced as a result of repeated moves from unit to unit or district to district, or whether these same officers are being sent to different locations as a result of repeated misconduct and essentially becoming spreaders of bad behavior.

Like all people, police officers are subject to peer influence within social network interactions, and it has been found that the informal types of these interactions are particularly powerful. If there is a way that these interactions can be leveraged for the dispersion of compliance, positive conduct, and accountability, instead of being used to diffuse misconduct and deviant behavior, then real gains in policing can be made. This is not only beneficial at the theoretical level but will result in very tangible improvements, for example, in officers feeling comfortable to step in to serve, protect, and save the life of George Floyd.

As an emerging field, network science capitalizes on the often overlooked social network as the level of analysis. It takes into account individual and institutional forces in the assessment of human behavior. Findings from studies can assist in producing policy change and correcting practices within policing. Table 2 provides a summary of findings from select studies.

2.3 Cocreation and Coproduction

Cocreation and coproduction refer to instances where providers work alongside consumers to create or design and produce or deliver a service or program (Brandsen & Honingh, 2018; Osborne, Strokosch & Radnor, 2018). These

Table 2 Network science and policing summary

Authors	Findings
Wood, Roithmayr & Papachristos, 2019 Börner, Sanyal & Vespignani, 2007	– Network science is an emerging area of research situated between individual and structural levels of analyses. – Network science develops theoretical and practical techniques to increase our understanding of naturally occurring human-made networks.
Papachristos, 2011	– Social networks, and specifically a person's placement within them, can impact outcomes related to criminality and delinquency.
Fagan, Wilkinson, & Davies, 2007	– Violent behavior can be effectively passed from person to person through forms of contact or interaction.
Green, Horel & Papachristos, 2017	– Models that incorporated social contagion and individual demographic information better predicted gunshot subjects than models that used those factors independently.
Roithmayr, 2016 Savitz, 1970	– Police are most strongly socialized in informal network settings, informing their perception of misconduct and deviant behavior.
Getty, Worrall & Morris, 2016 Ouellet et al., 2019 Quispe-Torreblanca & Stewart, 2019	– Field training officers (FTOs) can account for up to one-quarter of the variation in new police officers' allegations of simple misconduct, which then can be extended to use of force.
Zhao & Papachristos, 2020	– Officers who shoot are often characterized as being network brokers, meaning they occupy positions directly connecting otherwise disconnected parts of networks.

constructs speak to the value that customers or consumers add to a product or service in terms of its design and delivery (Vargo & Lusch, 2006). Though most authors agree on these sorts of broad definitions, there is no universally agreed-upon definition as to what cocreation or coproduction is. However, both concepts are associated with social innovation – a process that is dependent upon the active involvement or participation of residents of a community in the design and delivery or implementation of a public service (Voorberg, Bekkers & Tummers, 2015).

Cocreation and coproduction are often conducted without being explicitly mentioned and in some instances come about naturally. Coproduction and cocreation have long existed in the academic field but have recently seen a resurgence in popularity (Ostrom, 1990; Grönroos, 2012; Brandsen & Honingh, 2018; Osborne et al., 2018; Dudau et al., 2019). This rise in conjoint responsibility between residents or lay actors of a community and its governmental agents or state actors (Nabatchi, Sancino & Sicilia, 2017) may be popular due to its relevance to many new areas of academic research and policy, especially those that demand addressing existing social problems and the current political and societal unrest in the United States. The more people are displeased with public problems and how they are being handled by public officials, the more they become motivated to participate in cocreation and coproduction. These activities, often at the behest of governmental efforts, promote a civic culture and democratic values (Alford & Hughes, 2008).

Coproduction can be broken down into subsections like cocommissioning, codesign, codelivery, and coassessment (Bovaird & Loeffler, 2013); coproduction, codesign, and cocreation (Dudau et al., 2019); or coplanning, codelivering, and comonitoring (Uzochukwu & Thomas, 2018). These subsections take the broader concept of coproduction and break it down into manageable and more easily definable parts. This helps researchers add more specificity to their study and better explain what they are investigating.

Research on coproduction often follows a specific topic like coproduction in health care (some in Brandsen et al., 2018; Gheduzzi et al., 2020), in education (some in Brandsen et al., 2018), for environmental action (Alonso et al, 2019), or, most commonly, community involvement with public services (Brandsen et al., 2018; Uzochukwu & Thomas, 2018; Dudau et al., 2019). This coactivity reflects "a shift from 'public services *for* the public' toward 'public services *by* the public'" (Bovaird & Loeffler, 2013).

Some authors are more critical of the coproduction process and its claims (Gheduzzi et al., 2020; Dudau et al., 2019; and more). In literature that discusses the term codestruction, "almost all the definitions agree on considering codestruction to be an 'interactional process' in which different stakeholders are involved and fail to integrate each other parties' resources, reducing the well-being of one or more stakeholders" (Gheduzzi et al., 2020; Plé & Cáceres, 2010). In simpler terms, coproduction improves all groups' well-being while codestruction worsens at least one group's well-being. The considerable literature on codestruction exists as a response to the view that coproduction is a "panacea" for all public service concerns (Bovaird & Loeffler, 2013; Dudau et al, 2019). Gheduzzi et al. (2020) found four main causes of failure with coproduction: insufficient trust, mistakes, inability to serve by service providers, and the inability to change by service users. If each of these pitfalls is successfully avoided, codestruction will likely not occur and coproduction will produce a valuable result.

Alonso et al.'s (2019) analysis of what factors influence a person's participation in coproduction yielded sets of demographic, personality, and organizational characteristics that increase their involvement. Although their study focused on environmental action and not community involvement with issues of race and policing, the characteristics defining a highly coproductive individual are likely applicable. They found that rural dwellers, university graduates, women, and middle-aged individuals participated in coproduction more than the average person. Besides these demographic influences, three personal attitudes enhanced coproduction: self-efficacy, civic engagement, and being compassionate, along with three organizational attributes: the compatibility of public organizations with citizens' participation, the attitude of public officials toward citizens' participation, and the administrative culture (Alonso et al., 2019). This knowledge of factors that increase the success of coproduction will prove incredibly beneficial to discussions of whether a coproductive format will thrive across demographic groups.

In a similar analysis, Uzochukwu and Thomas (2018) found two patterns that impact people's willingness to participate in coproduction: political participation and citizen-initiated contacting of public officials. Their study found that psychological and social factors were reported as being most important for involvement in coproduction. This underscored the need for internal motivation for action. Another noteworthy observation from Uzochukwu and Thomas's (2018) research is the altruistic aspect to coproduction. People didn't engage for purely selfish motivations but instead cared about other members of their community and aspired that their community as a whole succeed. This finding provides encouragement for current and future endeavors into coproduction as a possible solution to public concerns.

Despite the research that has been conducted regarding cocreation and coproduction, there are gaps remaining to be investigated. Table 3 provides a summary of findings from select authors.

Table 3 CoCreation and coproduction summary

Authors	Findings
Alonso et al., 2019	– Distinct demographic, personality, and organizational qualities increase an individual's participation in coproduction.
Bovaird & Loeffler, 2013	– Coproduction has pros and cons, but it remains a positive addition to public service.
Brandsen et al., 2018	– Sections define, analyze, and investigate coproduction throughout different areas and domains.
Dudau et al., 2019	– Coproduction is often valued too highly in public service spaces, and the field is broadening, which presents new opportunities and challenges.
Gheduzzi et al., 2020	– Cultural differences in researchers may cause issues, but aspects of cocreation and codestruction can coexist, and codestruction is not inevitable.
Uzochukwu & Thomas, 2018	– Political participation and citizen-initiated contacting are key factors in successful coproduction.
Williams et al., 2016	– For coproduction to be effective, there must be an attitude shift and more frequent positive interactions between students and police, bringing the groups together.

3 The Interplay of Race, Policing, and Public Governance

3.1 An Examination of the Past

America's past is one that reflects challenges and difficulties due to the social construction of race. In theory, America was founded on the lofty principle that all men are created equal, but in reality, the country was conceived as an enslaving society. Racial profiles emerged along the color spectrum that resulted in biased beliefs and actions, discriminatory public policies, oppressive professional practices, and menacing social norms and actions. This conundrum resulted in an American dilemma (Myrdal 1944) and foreshadowed the significant, lasting myth and resulting problem of equating difference with deviance.

3.1.1 The Genesis and Legacy of Black Crimmythology

Race is a historical construct, yet it continues to have a contemporary impact on societies, in general, and American society, in particular. Race, as a social construction – an idea that has been created, accepted, and embraced by people within a society – is associated with three dimensions: a relative ease in identifying the "other," an immutable quality, and social consequence or outcome of this designation (Loury, 2002). The concept of race is reinforced by another social construct: stigma. Stigma is a physical sign that exposes something suspicious, strange, and negative about the moral status of the signifier (Goffman, 1963). Resultingly, the stigma of race and its perceived criminality have converged within the American context and arguably across the globe.

Race in American society is visual, apparent, and explicit. However, racism that emerges from the social construction of race can be hidden, covert, and insidious. Both race and racism are ever present, with the former being more visible and the latter, at times, less so. For example, the use of linguistic metaphors in the American context highlights the complementary nature of race and racism. Even though race matters and is more obvious to the eye, racism in some of its forms, like the use of linguistic metaphors, is more obscure but real. Recently, Aradhna Krishna posed a pertinent question: How did white become a metaphor for all things good?[11] This question gets at the embeddedness of race and racism in the US context.

Metaphors aid in sensemaking (Hill & Levenhagen, 1995; Patriotta & Brown, 2011). They serve as a cognitive tool that allows one to comprehend what they cannot perceive, hear, taste, or touch. Previous research has found that the color white is implicitly linked to goodness and morality, while the color black is conjoined with immorality – things that are devious or evil (Meier, Robinson & Clore, 2004). The use of linguistic metaphors has also impacted societal sensemaking of criminality and who is innately inclined to engage in illicit activities.

The color black is associated with criminality or villainous behavior and is entrenched in American lore. From the bad guy wearing the black cowboy hat in western movies of years past to present-day depictions of the Grim Reaper dressed in black, "the bad as black effect" is a part of the psychosocial beliefs of American society (Alter et al., 2016). This effect goes beyond the color of clothing to the color of one's skin. A myth called black crimmythology emerged that equated blackness and criminality, a concept offered by Billy Close (1997). Black crimmythology is based on numerous faulty fables and pseudoscientific facts that have been generated by racist, misguided individuals to support the notion of innate, black criminality. This "sensemaking" approach to mythmaking

---

[11] Aradhna Krishna (2020). How did "white" become a metaphor for all things good? *The Conversation.*

has had a snowball effect across generations of American society, with debilitating results for African Americans.

Black crimmythology within the American context can be traced to the efforts of sacred and secular institutions. The faith community of the past and not-so-distant past assisted in shaping and reinforcing the opinions of the selective white public, creating and projecting a racial profile that equated blackness with wrongdoings. The Hamitic myth (see Genesis 9:22–26) presented in the story of Noah and his son Ham has been used to justify the enslavement of African people. It served a devious purpose. It offered a theological expectation for deviant and criminal behavior of blacks to justify their enslavement (Fredrickson, 1981; Gabbidon, 2010). These erroneous interpretations and application of biblical text converged with the writings of so-called "learned" men who were educated by and affiliated with institutions of "higher" learning.

For example, Thomas Jefferson, [12] a "founding father" of the United States, the third president of the United States, and founder of the University of Virginia, along with other "thinkers" during the Enlightenment period like Immanuel Kant and David Hume, provided the scaffolding for the social construction of contemporary racial ideology (Eze, 1997). Relatedly, Dr. J. H. Van Evrie (1861) wrote an essay titled "Negroes and Negro Slavery: The First, an Inferior Race – The Latter, Its Normal Condition." A decade later, in 1871 Dr. Samuel Cartwright published his essay, "The Prognathous Thesis of Mankind." Both publications sought to prove that Negroes were biologically inferior to Caucasians, incapable of major advancement, and inherently savage. Consequently, Cartwright and Van Evrie advocated that subservience was the "natural and beneficent state" of the Negroes. These men utilized the scaffolding of earlier thinkers to build and reinforce a color-coded system of injustice.

Equating difference with deviance in the context of black crimmythology was not solely an American phenomenon. Black crimmythology traverses continents and cultures (Kalunta-Crumpton, 2010; Majavu, 2020). The Italian "scholar" Cesare Lombroso, who is often credited with being the father of criminal anthropology, published *The Criminal Man* in 1876, in which he postulated that there were four types of criminals: atavistic, insane, occasional, and impassioned (Lombroso et. al. 2006). Lombroso advanced the notion that blacks were atavists – born criminals, primitive throwbacks, and least evolved of all races. As such, they represented the most likely race of people to be involved in deviant or criminal behavior requiring disparate mechanisms for

---

[12] Conor Cruise O'Brien, 1996. Thomas Jefferson: Radical and racist. *The Atlantic.*

punishment without the hope of rehabilitation. Other scholars in criminology, sociology and related fields, like Park & Burgess (1924) and Reuter (1927), also shared the beliefs of Lombroso, Van Evrie, and Cartwright.

These views of the past have been transmitted across generations via print and audiovisual sources of media (Gilliam et al., 1996; Blendon & Young, 1998; Muharrar, 1998; Smiley & Fakunle, 2016; Oshiro & Valera, 2018). Modern platforms, like social media, continue to reinforce this historical narrative (Intravia, Thompson & Pickett, 2020). Post–Trayvon Martin, Michael Brown, George Floyd, and others, the promotion of those messages through these platforms is now being challenged (De Choudhury et al., 2016). Counternarratives are appearing that seek to cast light into the dark web.

Past beliefs, policies, societal, and professional practices within America, particularly those historic harms that affected people of color, still have a presence in the present. The legacy of stigma that accompanied race in the socially constructed and politically reinforced American society of yesterday continues to cast a foreboding shadow today in terms of black crimmythology. The artist Dave[13] intones that black is beautiful and black is excellent, but black pain is also evident due to the condemnation of blackness (Muhammad, 2019. This conundrum offers an opportunity to explore racism as systemic, structural, and institutionalized.

3.1.2 Discussion of Racism: Systemic, Structured, and Institutionalized

Race and racism are two concepts that are incredibly more complex and intertwined within the fibers of the United States than most Americans under-stand. A misunderstanding of race inevitably leads to a misunderstanding of racism, which inevitably leads to a misunderstanding of the implications of both. Though unfortunate, this sequence of events is extremely common. When racism is reduced to only flagrant bigotry and symbols of hate like the Ku Klux Klan, many are led to seemingly well-intentioned but simultaneously very harmful approaches to race and combating racism such as "not seeing color." The problem with this is that it causes an individual who does not see color to not see race as the very real factor it is, with real implications for real people. Likewise, putting the spotlight solely on blatant acts of racism causes the more unseen, but arguably more harmful, effects of systemic racism to remain unnoticed, underappreciated, and without correction.

Systemic racism is a plague that infects every fiber of America's being. Commonly referred to as institutionalized racism or structural racism, the idea refers to how American society reflects white supremacy and its corresponding

---

[13] Dave, 2019. "Black."

forms of oppression and privilege in every facet and every system of life (O'Dowd, 2020). These systems include but are not limited to government and legislation, the criminal justice system, education, and employment and hiring. Systemic racism holds black Americans back at the starting line, while their white counterparts walk, sprint, or leisurely jog ahead. In discussing systemic racism, it is important to differentiate it from other forms of racism and oppression.

Products of systemic racism include explicit and implicit bias. Explicit bias is in many ways the tip of the iceberg, taking the form of what most first think of when they think of racism: slurs, derogatory comments, and unabashed hateful feelings. Implicit bias, on the other hand, is the concept that the ideology of white supremacy can be so deeply entrenched within a person that their unconscious minds are dictating decisions and actions that are fundamentally racist, though that same person may never explicitly or consciously express an outright racist sentiment. However, simply because something was not done with bad intention or the purpose of causing harm does not exonerate that very action from being harmful or rooted in bias or racist ideology.

Two other ideas that are important to consider and aid in better understanding systemic racism are covert and overt racism. Covert racism and overt racism can respectively be thought of as being indirect versus direct or hidden versus apparent forms of racism (Coates, 2007). Not to be mistaken, one form is not necessarily "better" than the other. The aims of covert racism are the same as those of overt racism, though the tactics used are often subtle, subversive, and disguised as seemingly more palatable reasons for achieving the same underlying racist mission. The distinction between covert and overt racism points to the important idea within systemic racism that just because a behavior is not blatantly exposed doesn't mean it's not there or its consequences are not felt. Before you could outrightly deny a person employment on the grounds of their race, but now perhaps an unfamiliar name – one that is less traditionally white and therefore deemed less comforting, professional, or appealing – causes the application of an equally qualified black candidate to suddenly slip to the bottom of the stack (Bertrand & Mullainathan, 2004).

This is precisely where systemic racism comes in. It is a structure that envelopes everyone in racist and discriminatory policies and practices. As alluded to, one of the features of systemic racism is that it has a foundation in the law. In the United States, slavery was a legally sanctioned practice, three-fifths was the compromise that, by law, made a man worth less than a whole, and when slavery was finally legally abolished, the Thirteenth Amendment gave rise to a period of mass incarceration in order to take its place. These were the laws of the land that set the foundation for the creation of obstacles for millions of black Americans to overcome. Though formally abolished, the remnants are still present in surviving ideologies that themselves produce more impacts and implications to contend with. Generations following those who were directly affected by slavery and ensuing practices are still feeling its strong ripple effects.

In the United States, systemic racism still commonly pervades structures thought of as having broken free from the grasp of racism and discrimination. The education system is a system where this misperception is clearly illustrated. *Brown* v. *Board of Education* was a landmark ruling aimed at reversing the structural inequities brought about by state-sanctioned racial segregation in public schools. In the words of Chief Justice Earl Warren, "We conclude that in the field of public education the doctrine of 'separate but equal' has no place. Separate educational facilities are inherently unequal."

However, fast-forward to present day in the United States, and a close look will reveal that schools remain incredibly segregated. This is in part due to extremely vague language within the *Brown* v. *Board* decision ordering states to end segregation with "all deliberate speed." In some cases, this caused years, and even decades, to pass before steps were taken to comply with the decision. Additionally, at various locations the power of the decision was subsequently severely weakened after changes to laws regarding oversight were made (Ivan, 2020). Coinciding with this still-existent segregation is the fact that predominantly black and brown public schools receive substantially less funding and are extremely underresourced in comparison to predominantly white schools (Meatto, 2019). Black Americans turn to education to improve their economic circumstances because of the well-documented link between level of educational attainment and lifetime earnings (Card, 2005). Nevertheless, in spite of these efforts and this persistence, it has also been shown that white high school dropouts remain wealthier than black college graduates (Bruenig, 2014). These are the consequences and realities of systemic racism. One of systemic racism's most debilitating qualities is its ability to give the impression of progress through legislation and policy, when in fact not as much is improving in the communities these policies are aimed at affecting as perceived.

The fight to prosper within these systems of oppression has in many cases been a literal one. The living legacy of systemic racism is one that allowed Crispus Attucks to fight and die for the forthcoming idea of all men being created equal, which he would have been fundamentally denied the right to participate in. The legacy includes black veterans being denied GI Bill benefits post–World War II, the same benefits that would help their white comrades buy homes with guaranteed low-interest mortgages and receive education at universities across the country (Thompson, 2019). In those times the advancement of black people was characterized by fear that ultimately gave birth to the audacity to deny the rights of black Americans who fought to ensure that all Americans have the safety and liberty to enjoy those same rights.

Systemic racism is to triumph over hurdle after hurdle and still be met with another roadblock. It is to make it to the point where you've attained an education and all requisite qualifications, but your name keeps you from getting the job. Systemic racism is to overcome yet have centuries' worth of indoctrination to cause an officer to feel uneasy. All of this is reflected in the common sentiment within the black community that no amount of education, number of degrees, or level of respectability will save you when you are pulled over on the side of the road. That is the nature and reality of systemic racism, in all its forms and complexities, in this nation. This is America.[14] Systemic racism is embedded within the DNA and fabric of this country in its institutions, organizations, and agencies, including policing.

3.1.3 Policing: A Review of the Evolution of the American Experience

Law enforcement agencies in America, like other organizations, operate within an open-system environment (Katz & Kahn, 1971; Grandage, Aliperti, & Williams, 2018). They can influence and are influenced by individuals, institutions, mores, values, technologies, ideologies, and beliefs within their surroundings. As such, police departments and their officers are affected by political, social/cultural, technological, and other dynamics and adapt to environmental variations in order to provide the services that they have been tasked to deliver (Burns & Stalker, 2005).

Policing in America has evolved. Kelling and Moore (1988) described three eras of American policing: the political era – 1840s to the early 1900s; the reform era – the 1910s to the 1970s; and the community era from the 1980s to some would say the present. Gaines and Kappeler (2014) also offer a similar description but augment Kelling and Moore's description by adding a fourth era: the postcommunity policing era coupled with the rise of the surveillance state. What predates these eras are the old slave patrols of the colonial period of American society. During the colonial period, the need for surveillance was based upon the color of suspicion: being black. In essence, the more things changed within American society, it seems the more things stayed the same, especially in terms of black unbelonging (Jenkins, Tichavakuna & Coles, 2020).

Prior to receiving public funding and transitioning to the political era, early practices of social control were in place. These practices were informal and communal. Citizen volunteers and citizen-based watch groups were utilized to

---

[14] Childish Gambino, 2018. "This America."

ensure public safety, public order, and to maintain the status quo (Archbold, 2012). In colonial America, in general, and in the American South, in particular, slave patrols[15] were used to ensure the enforcement of racialized laws to maintain order (Berlin, 1976; Reichel, 1998). Slave patrols were first formed in 1704 in South Carolina (Hadden, 2001) and had three primary functions: (1) to chase down, apprehend, and return to their owners runaway slaves; (2) to provide a form of organized terror to deter slave revolts; and (3) to maintain a form of discipline for slave-workers who were subject to summary justice, outside the law (Potter, nd). Slave patrols are now considered the precursor of American law enforcement agencies. These patrols operated prior to and after the war of rebellion over slavery (Hadden, 2001; Websdale, 2001).

This initial policy and practice of public safety and public order created divisions during and beyond the emergence of a new country. These policies and practices ran contrary to the espoused individual freedoms and rights and was the antithesis of the professed principle that all men were created equal and enjoyed inalienable rights bestowed upon them by their Creator (Berlin, 1976; Archbold, 2012; Grandage, Aliperti & Williams, 2018). Despite the evolution of policing in America paired with the progress made within our society, a couple of constants seem to remain: the assumption of blackness with criminality and the unconscious/implicit bias that is most pronounced along racial lines (Weir, 2016). These two constants converge at the interplay of race, policing, and public governance. At this intersection lie issues related to use of force. A discussion follows that provides an excavation and exploration of this legal concept. Special attention is devoted to case law that serves as the structural design for this police policy and its resulting practice.

3.1.4 Graham v. Connor: *The Architecture of Police Use of Force – §1983*

To begin to understand the architecture of the US police excessive use of force doctrine one must conceptualize the underpinnings of the legal remedies afforded to individual citizens that have been assaulted by those governmental officers. The Civil Rights Act of 1871, also commonly known as §1983, provides a right of action (the ability to bring suit) for individuals who have been deprived of a right under the Constitution or law (42 USCA § 1983). In enacting the statue, Congress intended to give a remedy to parties deprived of their constitutional rights, privileges, and immunities by an official's abuse of their position and intended to override certain kinds of state laws, to provide a remedy where state law is inadequate, to provide a federal remedy where a theoretically adequate state remedy is not practically available, and to provide

---

[15] Chelsea Hansen, 2019. Slave patrols: An early form of American policing. *Blog: On the Beat.*

a federal remedy supplemental to existing state remedies. To garner recovery (win a favorable judgment) under §1983, a plaintiff alleging that a police officer used excessive force during an arrest must show that the force to which the plaintiff was subjected constituted a "deprivation of any rights, privileges, or immunities secured by the Constitution and laws" (42 USCA § 1983). Plaintiffs generally ground their claims in the Fourth Amendment, which provides protection from unreasonable searches and seizures (USCS Const. Amend. 4). Courts across variant circuits have enumerated their own standard for gauging the constitutionality of a police officer's excessive uses of force. Following the ruling in *Graham v. Connor* (1989), the use of unreasonable force during an arrest is a violation of constitutional rights. Under this standard the reasonableness of the use of force is gauged by the ordinary, prudent man. The reasonableness standard is further teased out in *Graham* and will be elaborated on in the coming sections.

3.1.5 Qualified Immunity: An Overview

When faced with a §1983 lawsuit, defendant police officers look to the legal doctrine of qualified immunity to shield their behavior from hefty monetary damages. Qualified immunity shields government officials from constitutional claims for money damages so long as the official did not violate clearly established law (Schwartz, 2017).

The Supreme Court has described the doctrine as incredibly robust and far-reaching – protecting "all but the plainly incompetent or those who knowingly violate the law" (Schwartz, 2017). The doctrine of qualified immunity is intended by the Court to "balance the need to hold government officials accountable when they exercise power irresponsibly and the need to shield officials from harassment, distraction, and liability when they perform their duties responsibly" (Schwartz, 2017). The Supreme Court first announced that law enforcement officials were entitled to a qualified immunity from suits in the case of *Pierson v. Ray* (1967). In that decision, the Court justified the qualified immunity extended to law enforcement officers as a means of protecting government defendants from financial burdens when acting in good faith in legally murky areas. The Court saw qualified immunity as necessary because "[a] policeman's lot is not so unhappy that he must choose between being charged with dereliction of duty if he does not arrest when he had probable cause and being mulcted in damages if he does" (*Pierson v. Ray*, 1967).

In evaluating claims of qualified immunity, a court must first decide whether the officer or officers violated the constitutional rights of individuals and then decide whether the constitutional right was clearly established such that it would have been clear to a reasonable officer that his conduct was unlawful in the situation (*Saucier* v. *Katz*, 2001). "Clearly established" for purposes of qualified immunity means that the contours of the right must be sufficiently clear that a reasonable officer would understand that what they are doing is violative of that right (Federal Law Enforcement Training Center, nd). During cases of police excessive use of force, it is likely that plaintiffs will ground their claims in the Fourth Amendment to ward off the defense of qualified immunity. For example, in *Brooks* v. *City of Seattle* (2010), the Ninth Circuit held that in the specific context of that case, it was constitutionally excessive to tase a pregnant woman three times in less than one minute. Despite this holding, the court still permitted the defense of qualified immunity because the law was not sufficiently clear for every officer to understand the wrongdoing (Federal Law Enforcement Training Center, nd). Even with this effort by plaintiffs, courts across the United States have been deferential to the actions of police officers just like the officers in *Brooks* (Brown, 1991) and, as such, rarely issuing judgements against police officers.

***Johnson* v. *Glick*.** In *Johnson v. Glick* (1973), Judge Friendly of the Second Circuit decided a § 1983 damages claim filed by a pretrial detainee who claimed that a guard had assaulted him without justification. In ruling, Judge Friendly established a subjective standard by which to analyze such excessive use of force claims under § 1983. The excessive force used must "shock the conscience" to violate the Fourteenth Amendment (*Johnson* v. *Glick*, 1973). To contextualize this amorphous, subjective standard, Judge Friendly established four factors ("*Glick* Factors") by which to analyze the claim of excessive force.

Australia Johnson, who had been held in the House of Detention prior to and during his trial in the state courts on felony charges, sued both the warden of the Manhattan House of Detention for Men and corrections officer John Fuller under § 1983 (*Johnson* v. *Glick*, 1973). While being checked back into the House of Detention, Officer Fuller reprimanded Johnson and other men for allegedly failing to follow instructions (*Johnson* v. *Glick*, 1973). Johnson then tried to explain that they were doing only what another officer had told them to do (*Johnson* v. *Glick*, 1973). While in the midst of explaining, Officer Fuller rushed into the holding cell, grabbed Johnson by the collar, and struck him twice on the head with something enclosed in the officer's fist (*Johnson* v. *Glick*, 1973). During the attack, Officer Fuller threatened him, saying "I'll kill you, old man, I'll break you in half." (*Johnson* v. *Glick*, 1973). Following the attack, Fuller harassed Johnson by detaining him in the holding cell for two hours before returning him to his cell. Fuller then went on to hold

Johnson for two more hours after Fuller was ordered to take Johnson to the jail doctor (*Johnson* v. *Glick*, 1973). Last, despite being given "pain pills" by the jail doctor, Johnson still had "terrible pains" in his head (*Johnson* v. *Glick*, 1973).

In ruling on this case, Judge Friendly walked through the case law regarding complaints of excessive force or brutality. Ultimately, Judge Friendly found that "[m]any of the opinions . . . rely on a passing reference to the 'cruel and unusual punishment' clause of the Eighth Amendment" (*Johnson v. Glick*, 1973). And furthermore, that "a case like this, however, does not lie comfortably within the Eighth Amendment" (*Johnson v. Glick*, 1973). Friendly took a narrow view of constitutional interpretation with respect to the Eighth Amendment – limiting it to legislative and judicial action on those that are convicted. Friendly went on to say that the "cruel and unusual punishment clause is [not] properly applicable at all until after conviction and sentencing" (*Johnson v. Glick*, 1973). Despite eliminating the Eighth Amendment as a source of protection for detainees, Friendly admitted that "it would be absurd to hold that a pre-trial detainee has less constitutional protection against acts of prison guards than one who has been convicted" (*Johnson v. Glick*, 1973).

Friendly ultimately held that constitutional protection against police brutality is not limited to conduct violating the specific command of the Eighth Amendment. Rather, Friendly widened the net by analyzing claims of police brutality under substantive due process. Friendly held that application of undue force by law enforcement officers deprives a suspect of liberty without due process of law. Friendly admits that the "shock the conscience" standard that had been used prior is not definable (Brown, 1991). In order to color the standard established in *Glick*, Judge Friendly offers four factors to determine the constitutionality of the use of force. "In determining whether the constitutional line has been crossed, a court must look to such factors as the need for the application of force, the relationship between the need and the amount of force that was used, the extent of injury inflicted, and whether force was applied in a good faith effort to maintain or restore discipline or maliciously and sadistically for the very purpose of causing harm" (*Johnson v. Glick*, 1973). These four elements are known as the *Glick* Factors.

Graham v. Connor. In *Graham* v. *Connor* (1989), Chief Justice Rehnquist decided the constitutional standard that governs a free citizen's claim that law enforcement officials used excessive force in the course of making an arrest, investigatory stop, or other "seizure" of his person. The Court held that these §1983 claims are "properly analyzed under the Fourth Amendment's 'objective reasonableness' standard, rather than under a substantive due process" standard as illustrated in *Johnson* v. *Glick* (*Graham* v. *Connor*, 1989).

On November 12, 1984, Dethorne Graham, a black diabetic man, felt the onset of an insulin reaction while working at a Charlotte, North Carolina, auto shop (*Graham* v. *Connor*, 1989). Knowing that glucose (sugar) worked as an agent to reverse the reaction, Graham asked his friend, William Berry, to drive him to a nearby convenience store to purchase some orange juice (*Graham* v. *Connor*, 1989). After noticing the long checkout line, Graham hurriedly exited the store and entered Berry's vehicle once again (*Graham* v. *Connor*, 1989). Following the hasty exit from the store, a Charlotte police officer, M. S. Connor, followed Berry's vehicle and subsequently made an investigative stop approximately one-half mile from the convenience store (*Graham* v. *Connor*, 1989). During the stop Berry explained to the officers that Graham was experiencing a "sugar reaction" (*Graham* v. *Connor*, 1989). Officer Connor then instructed Berry to wait while he determined what occurred at the convenience store (*Graham* v. *Connor*, 1989). While Officer Connor called for backup to the scene, Graham's condition worsened; he got out of the car and ran around it twice (*Graham* v. *Connor*, 1989). Graham was experiencing insulin shock, which is characterized by progressive deterioration of bodily functions beginning with sweating, tremors, anxiety, and vertigo (*Graham* v. *Connor*, 1989). If the insulin shock remains uncorrected, delirium, convulsions, and collapse can occur (Brown, 1991). After running around the car twice, Graham collapsed on the curb and awoke to handcuffs being placed on his wrists while he was lying face down on the ground. As the backup Charlotte police officers arrived on the scene, one remarked, "I've seen a lot of people with sugar diabetes that never acted like this. Ain't nothing wrong with the M. F. but drunk. Lock the S. B. up" (*Graham* v. *Connor*, 1989). Graham continued to plead with the officers to check his diabetes card in his wallet. The officers responded with "shut up" and shoved Graham's face into the hood of Berry's car (*Graham* v. *Connor*, 1989). One of Graham's friends brought orange juice to the car, but the officers disallowed Graham from drinking any (*Graham* v. *Connor*, 1989). Four officers then threw Graham into the back of a police car headfirst (*Graham* v. *Connor*, 1989). Finally, Officer Connor received word that Graham had done nothing wrong at the convenience store, and the officers drove him home and released him (*Graham* v. *Connor*, 1989). During the assault, Graham sustained a broken foot, cuts on his wrists, a bruised forehead, and an injured shoulder (*Graham* v. *Connor*, 1989). Graham also claims to have constant ringing in his right ear that continues to this day (*Graham* v. *Connor*, 1989).

After the attack, Graham then commenced an action under 42 USC §1983 against the individual officers involved in the incident, alleging that they had used excessive force in making the investigatory stop in violation of his rights afforded under the Fourteenth Amendment. The district court considered the following four *"Glick"* Factors: (1) the need for the application of force; (2) the relationship between the need and the amount of force that was used; (3) the extent of the injury inflicted; and (4) whether the force was applied in a good faith effort to maintain and restore discipline or maliciously and sadistically for the very purpose of causing harm. The district court held that the amount of force used by the officers was "appropriate under the circumstances," that "there was no discernable injury inflicted," and that the force used "was not applied maliciously or sadistically for the very purpose of causing harm" but in "a good faith effort to maintain or restore order in the face of a potentially explosive situation" (*Graham* v. *Connor*, 1989). The district court's decision was affirmed by a divided panel by the Court of Appeals of the Fourth Circuit. The majority affirmed the district court's legal standard, and the majority also endorsed the four-factor test applied by the district court as generally applicable to all claims of "constitutionally excessive force" brought against government officials (*Graham* v. *Connor*, 1989). The majority also went on to hold that a reasonable jury applying the four-part test "could not find that the force applied was constitutionally excessive" (*Graham* v. *Connor*, 1989).

In deciding the case, Chief Justice Rehnquist held that all claims of excessive force, deadly or otherwise, in the course of an arrest, investigatory stop, or other "seizures" of a free citizen should be analyzed under the Fourth Amendment and its "reasonableness" standard, rather than the substantive due process standard as illustrated by the four-part *Glick* test (*Graham* v. *Connor*, 1989). Chief Justice Rehnquist grounded this holding by establishing that the Fourth Amendment provides an explicit textual source of constitutional protection against this sort of physically intrusive governmental conduct. To properly address a §1983 excessive force claim, analysis begins by identifying the specific constitutional right allegedly infringed by the challenged application of force (*Graham* v. *Connor*, 1989). First, in any §1983 suit the Court must isolate the precise constitutional violation with which (the defendant) is charged (*Graham* v. *Connor*, 1989). For cases of police excessive use of force, this will likely be the Fourth Amendment, which protects against unlawful seizures. Then, the validity of the claim must be judged by reference to the specific constitutional standard that governs that right, not some generalized excessive use of force standard (Brown, 1991). For cases of police excessive use of force, this would be the reasonableness standard as illustrated in *Graham*.

3.2 The Impact on the Present in Black and White and on Blue

> "There is no greater power for change than a community discovering what it cares about."
>
> – Margaret J. Wheatley, *Turning to One Another* (2002)

It is clear that the deaths of George Floyd, Breonna Taylor, and others have powerfully impacted the current political climate and the minds of people in America and across the world. This current climate has created an unprecedented level of support[16] for the Black Lives Matter movement and has brought more people into the conversation of race, community, and policing than ever before. During two weeks in June 2020, American voters' support for the Black Lives Matter movement increased dramatically nearly as much as it had in the preceding two years (Cohn & Quealy, 2020). This moment of national and global attention presents itself as a unique opportunity for real and concrete change. In Margaret Wheatly's words, our collective communities have discovered what they care about and are ready to take action.

3.2.1 The Revelation of Public Opinion Data

Public opinion data offers an ideal platform for gathering the people's honest and unbiased opinions on current topics. Surveys and polls are chosen as research methods because they are a concise and methodological tool for collecting and interpreting a vast amount of data and because they allow for the quantitative measuring of different perspectives and the graphing of the results. The surveys and polls referenced in this section are from online websites that gather responses from the American people on a variety of topics; the surveys chosen for this section are those that pertain to race and policing.

3.2.2 Public Trust and Confidence in Law Enforcement and the US Criminal Justice System in Black and White

Several surveys that aim to analyze how public opinion has shifted during this tumultuous time have been conducted. This gathering of broad opinion proves useful for understanding the general consensus on a topic. A survey from the Democracy Fund and UCLA Nationscape Project[17] analyzed public opinion of the police from May 21–27, 2020, compared to May 28–June 3,

---

[16] Nate Cohn and Kevin Quealy, 2020. How public opinion has moved on Black Lives Matter. *The New York Times.*

[17] Rebecca Morin, 2020. Americans' perceptions of police drop significantly in one week as protests continue, survey finds. *USA Today.*

2020. This survey found that the percentage of favorable opinions of the police has decreased for all races represented, 47 percent to 38 percent of black respondents stating a favorable opinion and from 72 percent to 61 percent for white respondents (see Figure 1). Consequently, the percentage of unfavorable opinions of the police has increased for all races represented, from 44 percent to 54 percent of black respondents stating a negative opinion and from 18 percent to 31 percent for white respondents (see Figure 2).

ABC News and Ipsos published a poll[18] comparing public opinion on police killings from December 2014 to an ABC News and *Washington Post* poll from June 2020 on the same topic. When polled back in 2014 about Ferguson and New York City, 75 percent of black respondents believed that these events were representative of a greater issue while 60 percent of white respondents considered them to be isolated incidents. When polled in June 2020 about the death of George Floyd, 95 percent of black respondents, 70 percent of white respondents, and 74 percent of all adults agreed that this event was representative of a greater problem (see Figures 3 and 4). Not only has the current political climate around these tragedies brought more attention to police-community relations and race, but it has also drastically closed the gap in opinions, bringing people together and closer to a universal agreement that change must occur. In this world of increasingly polarizing

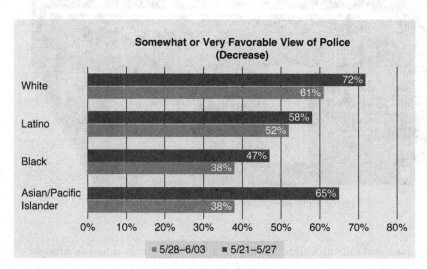

Figure 1 Public opinion of police by race - Decrease in positive views
Source: *Democracy Fund and UCLA Nationscape Project.*

---

[18] Chris Jackson and Mallory Newall, 2020. Americans overwhelmingly view Floyd killing as part of larger problem. Ipsos.

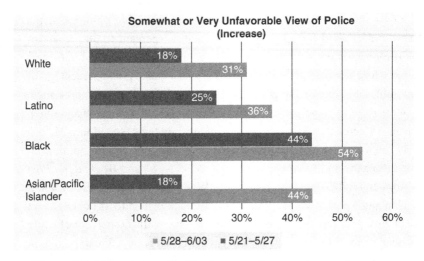

Figure 2 Public opinion of police by race - Increase in negative views
Source: *Democracy Fund and UCLA Nationscape Project.*

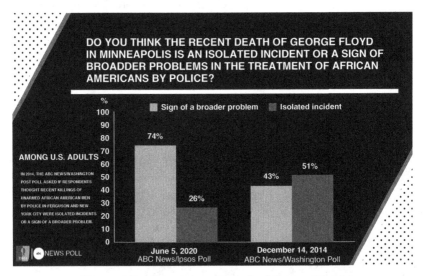

Figure 3 Public opinion on death of George Floyd

opinions and radicalization, the fact that this moment in time has brought people's opinions close to each other should not be overlooked.

The final survey[19] from public opinion site Civiqs asks whether respondents support or oppose the Black Lives Matter movement. The results show that

---

[19] Black Lives Matter, 2017–20. Civiqs.

Americans view Floyd killing as part of larger problem

Majorities across groups think Floyd's death is a sign of broader problems in the treatment of African Americans by police

Do you think the recent death of George Floyd in Minneapolis is an isolated incident or a sign of broader problems in the treatment of African Americans by police?

% A sign of broader problems in the treatment of African Americans by police

■ All Americans
■ African American
■ Hispanic
▨ White
▨ Democrat
▨ Republican

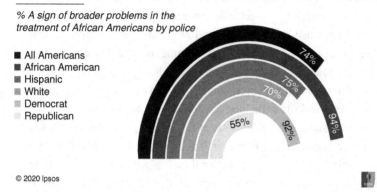

© 2020 Ipsos

Figure 4 Public opinion of Floyd's killing by police as sign of larger problem

although the percentage of people opposing the movement has been slowly decreasing since April 2017 when the results began, the movement received a drastic increase in support (and drastic decrease of opposition) at the end of May 2020, with a record amount of support at 53 percent from June 1–June 6. At that point the opposing percentage fell to only 28 percent. Since then, these numbers have adjusted to 50 percent in support and 34 percent in opposition as of July 7, 2020 (Civiqs.com). The 6 percent increase in opposition since its initial decline may possibly have been caused by extremists on either side and violent protests that swept the nation, while the 3 percent decrease in support might be the result of desensitization or a plateau in attention. However, both of these changes could simply be the result of minor adjustments, and it remains to be seen if and how public opinion continues to shift. The steep rise in support near the end of May might be attributable to the increase in knowledge on the topic from the news and social media. Many more people have been brought into the conversation and have therefore inspired others to follow suit. Another fascinating note to mention from this graph is that the percentage of people who neither supported nor opposed the movement was relatively constant from 2017 until the end of May, at which point the percentage of ambivalence fell to just 14 percent as of the last measurement on July 6. This statistic illustrates how the Black Lives Matter movement has become much more well known and has gained a large amount of attention of late, leading to more people taking a stand.

3.2.3 Discussion of Impact on the Blue

From these survey results, it is clear that public opinion of police has significantly decreased. Attention has now been brought to the injustice and racism that plague black and brown communities, injustices that are committed by the hands of the very people who are sworn to protect. The American people's eyes have been opened, and they have had enough. A second poll from Ipsos[20] revealed that although the vast majority of Americans support some sort of police change, just 34 percent of Americans supported defunding the police – 57 percent of black respondents and 26 percent of white respondents – when results were distributed by race (see Figures 5 and 6). Defunding the police is a cry often voiced by the public that calls for a significant reallocation of funds from police departments to other public service organizations. However, it is important to consider that such a call may not entirely address the institutional racism within policing and the public opinion that supports resulting violence. While greater funding of public service organizations and agencies aimed at improving housing, education, recreation, and mental health services likely would decrease crime, violence, and delinquency, removing funds from police departments could contribute to a worsening of the quality and conditions of policing by not directly confronting

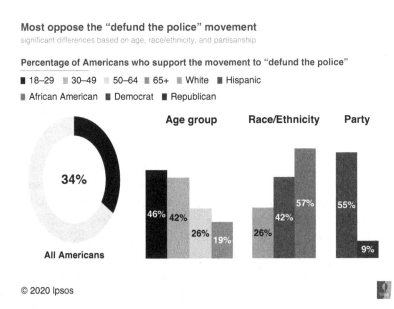

© 2020 Ipsos

Figure 5 Most oppose defunding the police movement

---

[20] Sarah Feldman, 2020. Americans agree with police reform, but defund the police currently a bridge too far. Ipsos.

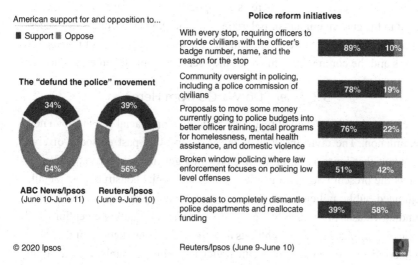

Figure 6 Support for police reform but opposition to defund movement

the historic and structural racism within the profession. Even with fewer funds, an institution that is systemically racist will continue to be systemically racist until it is intentionally reconstructed. This illuminates why it is important to tackle the problems that plague policing head-on.

Although a binary option between funding the police or funding other public service organizations and agencies is often presented, a creative public policy approach could see both aims met. Thus, the outcomes of this poll are intriguing and the results are clear: The public is demanding significant change from law enforcement agencies, but the majority do not believe that defunding the police is the way to promote such change. This proof of the national support for change within policing but also change alongside policing is promising. There is a history of injustice in this country, both explicit and implicit, and now is the time that those injustices must be rectified. The past and the present have aligned to create this moment that will define our collective future.

Current events have caused people to think significantly less favorably of police and support significant organizational revision. Although this might initially seem like it will have a negative impact on the blue, it should be seen as the exact opposite. At this unique moment in time, all attention is on law enforcement agencies and how they respond to the movement as people are in agreement that change must occur. This presents a unique opportunity: Public attention is focused on the issues around the police, and the American people support taking action. This gives law enforcement agencies the chance to take the advice given to them by experts and create new dialogues and programs alongside their community. There is an opportunity now, which is unprecedented in the current climate of polarizing opinions and dividedness, for necessary and tangible changes to occur with the support of the people for both police officers and the communities in which they serve to come together and heal.

3.3 Where Do We Go from Here?

The current dystopian state of relational policing along racial lines is not a new phenomenon. The civil unrest of today is a repeat of past episodes of civil discontent that have flared up during previous generations. Past episodes, as well as the present one, are a result of erroneous social constructions, racially prejudiced public policies, and discriminatory policing practices. These compounding catastrophes have had a negative impact on public perceptions and public institutions. Figure 7 highlights how the social constructions of race have led to political constructions or public policies that impact public organizations like police departments. These policies become embedded within the professional practices of those public servants and ultimately affect public perception.

Figure 7 Impact of social constructions

Lessons have not been learned and teachable moments have not been taken advantage of in the past. So, where do we go from here? This question is explored by taking a brief look back at some lost opportunities and resulting opportunity costs to make improvements and address the historic harms that continue to menace present-day police-community relations.

3.3.1 Opportunity Costs and Opportunities Lost

In the US context, there have been numerous occasions to learn from mistakes that have negatively affected police-community relations. These failures to adequately react, reform, and revise police policies and practices represent lost opportunities. We use a recent article by Headley and Wright (2019) as a guide to highlight the opportunities to reduce excessive police use of force and build police-community relations. We pay particular attention to four US police commissions: the Wickersham Commission in 1931, the Kerner Commission in 1968, the President's Task Force on 21st Century Policing in 2015, and the US Commission on Civil Rights Report on Police Use of Force in 2018.

The National Commission on Law Observance and Enforcement, or the Wickersham Commission (1931), was the first federal assessment of law enforcement in the United States. The Wickersham Commission was established during the presidential administration of Herbert Hoover. The Wickersham Commission Report was published in 1931, and its primary focus was on the national alcohol prohibition. Additional attention was also given to issues of police corruption, excessive use of force, and abuse of power. These issues impacted public trust and public confidence in policing and set in motion proposed recommendations to improve the profession, its practices, and the US criminal justice system (Wickersham Commission, 1931).

In 1968, under the presidential administration of Lyndon B. Johnson, the National Advisory Commission on Civil Disorder, or the Kerner Commission, was established. This commission was in response to the protests and unrest occurring in communities of color across the United States around race relations during the civil rights movement (National Advisory Commission on Civil Disorders, 1968). The Kerner Commission Report was released and formally acknowledged the difficulties of the lived experiences of blacks when compared to whites. The report emphasized twelve deeply held grievances that affected the civil unrest. These grievances included police practices, unemployment and underemployment, substandard housing, inadequate educational opportunities, poor recreational programs and facilities, ineffective infrastructure to voice grievances and effectively engage in the political process, condescending and disrespectful white attitudes, racialized and disparate administration of justice, inadequate federal programs, and inadequate municipal services. This finding illuminated to many the past injustices and systemic socioeconomic disadvantages of being black in America, which left their communities stigmatized, marginalized, and vulnerable. In essence, the report found that instances of police brutality were the antecedents for many of the riots in urban communities. Like the Wickersham Report, recommendations were made to address the problems that were faced (National Advisory Commission on Civil Disorders, 1968).

In 2015 the President's Task Force on 21st Century Policing (2015) was established under the presidential administration of Barack Obama. This task force, like the Kerner Commission, was a result of civil unrest following officer-involved shootings of African Americans. It focused on six pillars: building trust and legitimacy, policy and oversight, technology and social media, community policing and crime reduction, training and education, and officer safety and wellness. It offered recommendations and devised a strategy to facilitate the movement of those recommendations into action. In particular, the implementa tion guide[21] provided five ways for the three stakeholder groups (local government, law enforcement, and communities) to implement its recommendations (President's Task Force on 21st Century Policing, 2015).

The most recent reform effort is the 2018 US Commission on Civil Rights. Established under the presidential administration of Donald J. Trump, this commission investigated police use of force, with particular attention given to whether rates and instantiations of that use of force violated civil rights of persons of color, persons with disabilities, LGBT communities, and low-income persons. It sought to identify promising or proven policies and practices worth replicating to minimize unnecessary use of force to address the perception and reality of discrimination in police use of force (US Commission on Civil Rights, Office of Public Affairs, 2018). Their analysis, titled Report on Police Use of Force: An Examination of Modern Policing Practices, highlighted the importance of police professionalism, independent oversight and investigations, accountability, transparency, building police-community relations, national public record keeping on use of force, and officer training (US Commission on Civil Rights, Office of Public Affairs, 2018).

The aforementioned task forces or commissions identified similar systemic problems and recommended solutions with regard to policing. These solutions included, but were not limited to, the need for trust, accountability, transparency, improved community relations, improved relations with the media, and better

---

[21] COPS Office, 2015. President's Task Force on 21st Century Policing Implementation Guide: Moving from Recommendations to Action. Washington, DC: Office of Community Oriented Policing Services.

training and education standards for officers. These recommendations were offered but have yet to be fully operationalized. These lost opportunities have resulted in opportunity costs – suboptimal return on investments or the missed benefits due to making a bad decision. To many individuals within the American mosaic, these losses in terms of opportunities and costs impact their perception and opinion of police officers and the profession of policing. These perceptions further advance America toward two societies: one black, one white – separate and unequal (National Advisory Commission on Civil Disorders, 1968).

3.3.2 Opportunity for Public Governance

Despite the aforementioned lost opportunities and resulting costs, opportunities are still open to public governance efforts. These efforts will require a different orientation – a shifting away from the traditional "power over" approach of government toward an embracing a "power with" approach to public governance. This shift is dependent upon finding a suitable equilibrium between traditional state actors and emerging lay actors that are part and parcel of the current efforts to cocreate policies, practices, and programs that coproduce public safety, public order, and community well-being.

Governance or public governance represents a new mode of governing that differs from the traditional, government-centric, hierarchical control model (Mayntz, 2003). Public governance is relational; it is concerned with the cocreation of policy (policy formulation or development) and the coproduction and codelivery of services (policy implementation) by state and lay actors (Nabatchi, Sancino & Sicilia, 2017). It requires a balancing of power between stakeholders within a networked society (Bovaird, 2005). In essence, public governance is dependent upon effective communication that leads to the cooperation, coordination, and collaboration to address a shared problem that faces the environment of the state and lay actors involved in this process.

Harmonizing in such a way is reliant upon a departure from traditional power-over approaches to government and arriving at a power-with destination of governance. This journey demands leveraging the art of getting things done with the assistance of people (Follett, 1998). It requires the giving up of power by state actors and the reception and acceptance of power by lay actors. This brings into focus Arnstein's (1969) ladder of civic participation.

Power-with implies more of a partnership or sharing of power and responsibility among state actors or regular creators and producers with lay actors or community cocreators and coproducers. In some instances, delegated power where community members have dominant decision-making authority may be needed. This type of civic participation and empowerment, like partnership, will be subject to negotiation between state and lay actors (Arnstein, 1969). Both partnership and delegated authority rungs of the civic participation ladder are associated with integration and coactive power (Follett, 1998), two concepts that usher in Section 4: exploring the implications for the future on the other side of now.

4 On the Other Side of Now: Implications for the Future

4.1 Methodological Approach to Generating Implications

On the other side of now, what are the implications for a brighter future in terms of police-community relations? To explore this question, we took an elite interviewing approach to qualitative inquiry but within the confines and constraints of the COVID-19 pandemic.

Qualitative inquiry rests upon an inductive and holistic philosophical foundation (Creswell & Poth, 2016). This foundation allows for the exploration of human issues, including wicked problems that are complex and challenging. Our research team was an integral part of the exploratory process. As qualitative researchers, we served as quilt makers – taking what Denzin and Lincoln (2005) have described as a *bricoleur* or a quilt-making approach – using the material at hand and deploying strategies that fit our circumstance. Subsequently, our plan was an iterative one that required flexibility in terms of planning for and conducting elite interviews.

4.1.1 Elite Interviews

Elite interviews are discussions with purposeful members of a population that are chosen because of who they are and what position they occupy (Aberbach & Rockman, 2002). Even though there is no universally agreed-upon definition of the term elite, traditionally these types of interviews have been used to gain insight from people directly involved in a political process (Zuckerman, 1972). As a result, they provide a subjective account of an issue and serve as a useful method to study power (Conti & O'Neil, 2007).

Elite interviews are a cost-effective tactic to research. They can generate unique data that is reliable, valid, and beneficial in investigating the nuances and complexities of policies and politics (Beamer, 2002). Consequently, they have been a key tool of qualitative analysis and are a staple approach to excavate and understand things that are political in nature.

Elite interviewing is associated with some challenges (Aberbach & Rockman, 2002). These limitations include sampling, the reliability of the interviewee, related interpretational problems, the need to an elementary understanding of the focal issue, and asking questions that subjects may be uncomfortable answering (Kezar, 2003; Harvey, 2011).

4.1.2 Recruitment of Participants and Development of Questions

Members of the research team utilized their networks to identify and recruit key informants. These informants included leaders of professional associations, sitting and retired police executives, student leaders at secondary and postsecondary institutions, and community leaders of activist and advocate organizations, including local police foundations. This *rapport* process to recruit participants relied upon trust to project and create a harmonious relationship between the researchers and the informants or interviewees. This process is effective in sharing information (Spradley, 1979), especially in the context of research related to policing and criminal justice organizations (Williams et al., 2015).

In light of what has been described as a pandemic within a pandemic, the conjoining of COVID-19 and systemic racism, we sought to gain insights from purposeful elites – police professionals who seek to improve police-community relations, high school and college students who are passionate and actively involved in social justice causes, and community members who are advocating for ways to reimagine policing. In keeping with approaches to select a sample for a qualitative study, we went beyond convenience sampling to judgment or purposeful sampling (Marshall, 1996). This purposeful approach was augmented by incorporating a snowballing approach (Naderifar, Goli & Ghaljaie, 2017) where we asked those interviewed to identify others who might want to share their views on this salient topic.

Typically, elite interviews are face-to-face or telephonic. Due to the constraints related to COVID-19, we had to be creative and innovative. We utilized an amalgam of approaches to gain insights from key informants. This blend included Zoom sessions, an online platform, telephonic interviews, and email responses.

We collected the perspectives of elites on what is to come in terms of police-community relations. We asked three open-ended questions to supplement demographic information:

1. From your perspective, what are the current obstacles present that hinder establishing, maintaining, and sustaining an effective partnership between the public and the police?
2. From your perspective, what are the current opportunities present that can improve the partnership between the public and the police as we move toward the future?
3. Is police change needed? If so, in what particular areas and why?

These questions emerged after receiving feedback from a small cadre of police professionals, community members, and student leaders. We worded and ordered our questions based upon their assessments. This approach aligns with the recommendations of others (Marshall, 2005; Addington-Hall, 2007).

4.1.3 Data Breakdown and Analysis

Eighty-four (84) people participated in our study. The self-reported demographic makeup of participants included 51 (or 60.7%) males; 33 (or 39.3%) females; 43 (or 51.2%) blacks/African Americans; 32 (or 38.1%) whites/Caucasians; 4 (or 4.8%) Asians/Asian Americans; 3 (or 3.6%) as mixed; and 2 (or 2.4%) Latinos. Forty-five respondents (or 53.6%) were students, 20 (or 23.8%) were police professionals, and 19 (or 22.6%) were community members. Seven participants (or 8.3%) were between the ages of 16–17; 36 (or 42.9 %) between the ages of 18–22; 2 (or 2.4%) between the ages of 23–30; 3 (or 3.6%) between the ages of 31–40; 10 (or 11.9%) between the ages of 41–50; 13 (or 15.5%) between the ages of 51–60; 8 (or 9.5%) between the ages of 61–70; and 5 (or 6%) over the age of 70. Summary figures are included in Figures 8 through 11, respectively.

All responses were transcribed and made available to the members of the research team for analysis. Researchers engaged in a systematic process to reduce and sort the data, generate notes and observations, and identify representative quotes. A color-coding strategy was applied to assist with this effort.

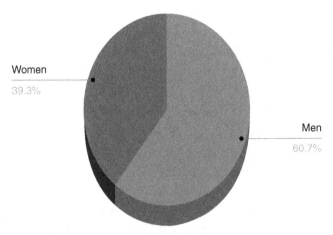

Figure 8 Gender of respondents

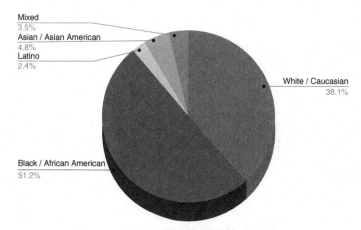

Figure 9 Race/ethnicity of respondents

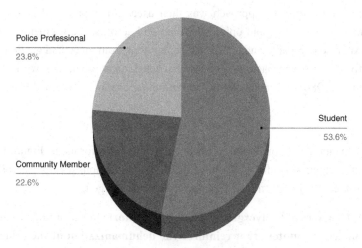

Figure 10 Status of respondents

These notes, observations, and quotes led to the generation of initial codes. This scheme was based on adapting a protocol offered by Knodel (1993).

Data from each elite interview were divided into three categories: key words, key phrases, and illustrative quotes of keen insights. To guide the analysis for surfacing themes, we utilized assertion analysis, which couples designation analysis (capturing the essence of the interviews by directly quoting informants) with attribution analysis (counting and coding the frequency of words, phrases, and statements) toward the identification of themes or perceptions.

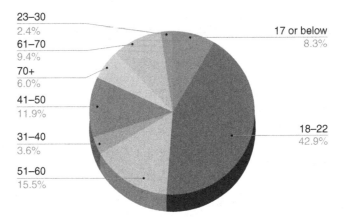

Figure 11 Age of respondents

A descriptive-interpretive approach was then used to compare and contrast perceptions, experiences, and opinions within and across the aforementioned groups. We also compared and contrasted perceptions from racial and gendered perspectives. This approach to content analyzed drew upon the work of Krippendorf (1980) and revealed the themes and perceptions described here.

4.1.4 Emergent Themes

Four dominant themes converged across our categories of informants. Figure 12 depicts these themes. Additionally, three themes or perceptions diverged across our categories. Strikingly, a salient observation also emerged.

Emergent Themes of Convergence: Theme 1 – Historic harms and contemporary police encounters that reinforce the dehumanization of the other. The first dominant theme highlights the impact of the historic relationship between police and people of color, coupled with the persistence of contemporary encounters that exude the perceived prevalence of excessive use of force. Recent, disturbing, and highly visible encounters seem to bolster the longstanding American narrative that dehumanizes and devalues the "other." The following quotes capture the sentiments that surfaced across all categories.

> The historical reality is that police were imagined as a force to maintain the status quo, which in the United States is Black oppression. They have never, and will never be the partner of communities of color because our progress is rooted in overturning the systems they are sworn to protect. As Black people attempt to break our metaphorical chains, police place us behind bars, and

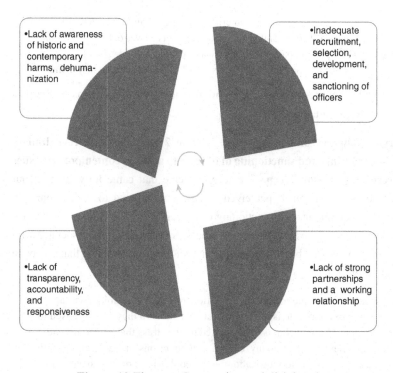

Figure 12 Themes: Converging and disjointed

because those missions are fundamentally inconsistent, partnership is unimaginable. America asks us to posit how police can surveil our communities in a more compassionate manner. Adding a pillow to our cage does not make police a partner in our success.

　　　　　　　　　　　　　– Vendarryl Jenkins, 26, black male law student

The policing profession seems to be unwilling to acknowledge its role in how people of color, especially African Americans, have been mistreated and marginalized by society. Law enforcement needs to publicly, candidly, and sincerely acknowledge how our history has undermined the present relationship between the police and communities of color.

　　　　　　　　　　　　　– Luke Bonkiewicz, white male police officer

There is a lack of accountability in police departments. Along with unjust laws, arrest quotas, over-policed communities, and vilified citizens, there is a culture of predatory policing.

　　　　　　　　　　　　　– Terrell Jana, black male college student

The police are seen as just one facet of a broader system of institutionalized racism, with the justice system heavily discriminating against minorities both historically and in the present.

　　　　　　　　　　　　　– William Fang, Asian male college student

Police were created to surveil and criminalize Black and other POC citizens within America. Their moniker of "protect and serve" was only meant for one group; white people, particularly rich white people.

– Sae'von Palmer, 21, black/Caribbean male community member

The preceding quotes reinforce the notion that the historic harms of the past have a presence in the present.

Emergent Themes of Convergence: Theme 2 – Inadequate recruitment, selection, training, and sanctioning of officers to address contemporary issues and resulting mission creep. The second theme that came forward from our analysis draws attention to perceived inadequacies related to the recruitment, selection, development, and sanctioning of officers. Informants noted that police officers engage in duties that go beyond what has been previously associated with local law enforcement, but officers do so without the proper training that is needed to be effective.

The police often understand their relationship with the public as antagonistic, where the public is the enemy rather than who they are supposed to be serving. I believe that is often caused by the stress that police are under because they serve so many community functions at once, alone with some unhelpful world views about why people are poor or in need in this country.

– Gustavo Moreira, 20, Latino male college student

Our police and judicial systems have allowed excessive violence and brutal behavior to go unpunished. Police protect their own and will rarely condemn an officer's actions publicly.

– Ephraim Reed, black male college student

Some departments have backed away from educational requirements for hiring because of the difficulty in filling positions; a bachelor's degree should be the minimum requirement for new officers given the ever increasing complexity of the work we ask them to do.

– Darrel Stephens, white male retired police executive

We need a more rigorous selection process for our law enforcement officers, and once they are in the program . . . the training must be vastly improved . . . to combat the ingrained habits within policing and the discriminatory policing that I have seen.

– Brian Zuluaga, Latino male, 2020 college graduate

Police are being asked to assume too much responsibility for too wide a variety of situations. Mental illness, homelessness, domestic violence, and other social ills are being handed off to undertrained and ill-equipped police officers.

– Karen Blair, white female community member

Training and trust. It is also difficult to build trust when officers lack the knowledge and skills of how to interact with those different from them. Balanced training that promotes and instills the value and importance of engaging with the public in a healthy way.

– Susan Del Prete, white female police professional

Establish more training for law enforcement on bias-based policing, culture diversity, community policing, DE-escalation training verbal judo, C.I. T. training, officer wellness, leadership training for mid-level and first-line supervisors, accountability with inclusion and transparency.

– Timothy Northern, African/Native American male police professional

Narrowing the scope of issues which police are being asked to address is a good step. Mental health professionals, counselors, negotiators, social workers among others may be helpful in addressing problems that police currently are asked to address.

– Talmadge Guy, African American male community member

Police do not have enough job training to effectively do their job. Police only have to do job training for 840 [hours] but barbers for 1,500. Police literally hold people's lives in their hands, their training should be longer and more detailed.

– Brandon White, African American male college student

Training . . . police do a very good job with tactical training but don't adequately address the human factor behind their decisions. Human life is reduced to statistics and percentages, when human life should be valued as human life.

– Thomas Thompson, white male police professional

This theme speaks to a general understanding that police officers' jobs are impacted by mission creep. Respondents across categories noted the need for additional efforts to recruit, select, and train efforts and accomplish the enlarged mission in addition to adequate sanctioning of officers that engenders public trust and confidence.

Emergent Themes of Convergence: Theme 3 – Lack of transparency as a reflection of lack of accountability and responsiveness. The third theme was a perception that police officers and departments were not accountable and responsive to the expectations of the public they serve. Respondents suggested that the lack of transparency reflected the police's unwillingness to accept what the public expected.

We need open complete transparency. Police are unable to be held accountable in a systematic and meaningful way. When they do bad things, there is no accountability and the public feel righteous anger. When the police see the backlash to their actions, they feel under attack and continue to mentally separate themselves.

– Confidential informant, African American male graduate student

Any partnership needs to have trust to be effective. In the eyes of the public, the police are not seen as trustworthy because they are not accountable in most cases.
                              – Gustavo Moreira, 20, Latino male college student

We all know that culture eats policy for breakfast. If it is acceptable to mistreat a person and little to no consequence is suffered for the mistreatment of people, that behavior will continue. Leadership has a responsibility to identify and stop misconduct as well as hold members accountable for unacceptable behavior.
                              – Bryant Hall, African American male police professional

The police profession doesn't need reform, it needs a sustained, ongoing commitment to evidence-based practices, community relationships, and accountability. Without this commitment, any reform is likely to be rashly implemented, poorly received by officers, and short-lived in both agencies and communities.
                              – Luke Bonkiewicz, white male police professional

This theme speaks to the need for transparency to serve as scaffolding to repair the damage done to relational policing efforts. Key informants suggested that by being more transparent, police departments would signal to the public their willingness to be more accountable and responsive to expectations.

Emergent Themes of Convergence: Theme 4 – The need to develop stronger relationships or partnerships between the public and the police. The final theme that emerged from our analysis was a need to develop stronger relationships between the public and the police. The following quotes provide some illustrative examples of this view.

Police-community collaboration.
                              – David Couper, white male retired police professional

[I]f there were more positive interactions between police and college students (black students) we would feel more comfortable with them . . . maybe a forum? Where students can directly talk with police without fear or judgment.
                              – Camryn Williams, African American female college student

[P]olice need to get more involved with the communities that they serve. Specifically, in black communities, there is already a distrust because most police don't live in those communities. If they did more work in the community and with the youth, I think that they would have a better understanding of the people they serve.
                              – Ephraim Reed, black male college student

Any programming that brings officers and police together whether it is through department events, foundation events, school offerings, community policing, etc. Communities and their governing bodies need to prioritize these programs, both in terms of time and money.
                              – Confidential informant, white female community member

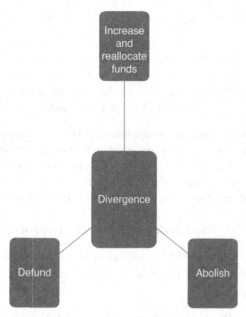

Figure 13 Diverging themes

I feel increased interaction within the community they serve will build trust. These could be in the form of police-hosted seminars on safety or even a PAL within the community. Interaction should not only be when assistance is needed.

– Dexter Johnigan, African American male community member

At the Parting: The emergences of three diverging themes. As depicted by Figure 13, three divergent themes surfaced from our analysis.

Emergent Themes of Divergence: Theme 1- Abolish the police. The first divergent theme was pronounced by students and community members who expressed a desire to abolish policing.

Police change is needed, but the change in question has to be defunction. The organization needs to be completely abolished, as Black people are being hunted down, and slain by the police.

– Sae'von Palmer, black/Caribbean male college student

The police need to be dismantled and abolished. The establishment of the police system rests upon a foundation of white supremacy, violence, and anti-blackness. There can be no effective partnership between communities of color (specifically black communities) and police because this

foundation hasn't been and cannot be removed from police departments
The police were not created to serve or protect the interest of black people.
— Kaksa Foskey, African American female community member

Operating under an abolitionist framework, I see opportunities for real
justice, healing, and safety when police are removed from the communities
that they harm and community-appointed leaders are given the task of
framing what health and security looks like for their communities.
— Rebecca Thompson, black female college student

We need an entirely new policing system. When a plant is poisonous you need it
removed, for it may harm the other plants around it. To remove it, you can't cut its
flowers and leave it there, for the roots and seeds still remain and history will
repeat itself. To remove a plant properly you must remove it from its roots, and
replenish the soil until it is time to plant a new plant which is beneficial to its
environment.
— Jayden Bolden, African American male college student

The theme of abolishment crossed racial and gender lines within the students
category. Within the community member category, this view was most preva-
lent by respondents of color.

Emergent Themes of Divergence: Theme 2 – Defund the police. The second
theme was more nuanced and expressed a desire to defund the police and reallocate resources to other human service areas, including housing, health care,
education, employment, and mental illness.

I believe that defunding the police and investing in communities will create
a healthier partnership between the public and police. Increasing funding for
education, housing, and public health will address issues such as poverty,
homelessness, and mental illness. If these issues are addressed properly,
police can focus more on "protecting and serving."
— Ephraim Reed, black/African American male college student

Redirect funding – use funds to help reduce police activity by increasing
funding to education, job programs, housing, mental health, etc.
— Roswell Lawrence, African American male community member

[Police change is needed] particularly in the ways they see their job as
Guardian vs. Warrior. Some defunding of police departments could be good
as well – if social services are willing to tackle more of the mental health,
homelessness, and domestic issues. Also, so many negative interactions take
place at traffic stops. What if unarmed traffic officers assumed those roles?
— Confidential informant, white female community member

This theme crossed racial/ethnic and age lines. But unlike the first divergent
theme, the call for defunding and reallocating resources was shared by students
and community members alike.

Emergent Themes of Divergence: Theme 3 – Increase funding and reallocate funds for policing efforts. The third theme of divergence was expressed by police professionals, both line and staff, male and female, as well as current and retired officers. Police officers and police executives as compared to students and community members saw a need to devote additional resources to efforts that improve relational policing and address mission creep.

> Defunding the police will exacerbate their ability to respond even more. Many have not recovered from the "Great Recession" and have already begun to take steps to deal with the loss of funding from the economic impact of COVID-19. To be sure – there needs to be a greater investment in social services, mental health treatment, substance abuse treatment, education, economic development.
> – Darrel Stephens, white male retired police executive

> Put more funding into community policing programs like P.A.L, G.R.E.A.T., Civic Leagues, community development programs, reaching out to high and middle schools and S.R.O.s reaching juveniles, establishing close relationships with positive outcomes.
> – Timothy Northern, African/Native American male police officer

> Whether to defund, re-appropriate funds or reorganize the department or to make a significant investment . . . I think there should be a significant investment. I think more emphasis is needed on service, more emphasis on education, more emphasis on training, and a recognition that the police officers are in a unique position to identify early on those social ills that are not being addressed. There needs to be enabling legislation that allows for more intervention in the areas of mental illness, homelessness.
> – Lou Dekmar, white male police executive

At the Merger of Divergence: A police culture that radiates community fear and distrust. The convergence of these themes seems to create a culture within policing that impacts the community that it serves. Respondents described a sense of fear and distrust due to the structural and systemic issues of race and racism within policing.

> The organizational structure and culture of policing is the largest obstacle. The police operate in a silo with an indoctrination process and cultural reinforcements to assimilate into police culture and identify as separate or different than community. Cultural reinforcements exist in the growth of police identity clothing, jewelry, flags, etc.
> – Wendy Stiver, white female retired police professional

> Unfortunately, the culture within many criminal justice agencies has formed an "us vs. them" mentality. This mentality often times dehumanizes aspects of the community, making it easier to disrespect people.
> – Bryant Hall, African American male police professional

To some key informants who are community leaders, the need to change the culture requires fresh, new leadership.

> Many of our police leaders either don't want or don't have the ability to push a culture of compassion to the street level officers. We likely need significant turnover in our leadership. We also need leadership that listens to the community and doesn't take the stance that police know how to fix their problems.
> – Thomas Thompson, white male community member

The perspectives expressed by the previous quote differ from a law enforcement leader who perceives this problem from his unique position as the former president of the International Association of Chiefs of Police.

> The challenges are much deeper than the police. I have a saying. "A community gets the police department that they deserve by the leaders they elect." Your police department is going to reflect the leadership of that community. If there is an issue with the police department, generally it is my experience that [it] is a symptom of a bigger problem. The focus is on the police department because the unique relationship that police have in any community ... [is] that the police is the enforcement arm of the government. As a result, its actions are amplified because of its relationship as a government actor and a citizen.
> – Lou Dekmar, white male police professional

Salient Observations: The growing power and influence of police unions. Two elite informants raised a salient point that resonates with many policing pundits: the growing power and influence of police unions.

> Police unions ... I think they have been an impediment to change in a lot of places. Again, not all – they're weak in some states, and maybe reasonably professional and progressive in some places. I reflect on the origin of unions in general – protecting the rights of workers from their bosses, who sometimes were unfair. Some of what we see in police unions is still that, a belief that they are at the mercy of their bosses (and politics) and looking for some protection. But many have taken that too far, and in addition become political themselves – definitely. Police union bosses all seem to be white guys – even in places where the police ranks are pretty diverse. It would be a big help if women police and Latino police and Black police somehow got control of their unions.
> – Confidential informant, white male retired police executive

> We need ... police accountability in serious, departmental, and systematic ways ... strong whistleblower protections and destruction of police unions entirely, as they often act not in labor interests of police but instead in destroying accountability mechanisms.
> – Confidential informant, black male graduate student

The collective bargaining agreements secured by unions shield police from being accountable to departmental and public expectations (Bies, 2017; Rushin, 2017).

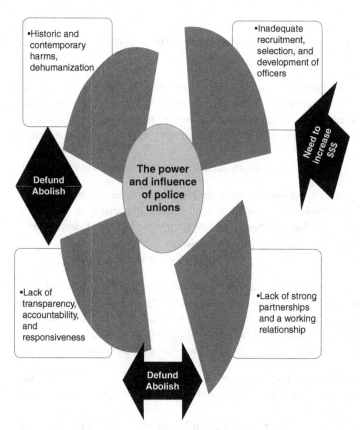

Figure 14 Converging and diverging themes

The perspectives of these elite informants highlight the need for internal leadership to better address the contemporary challenges that police unions pose. A growing number of others underscore the need for external oversight and control[22] by elected officials. To some, police unions are now identified as one of the biggest obstacles[23] to reform. Figure 14 depicts the impact of the converging and diverging themes, coupled with the salient observations.

At the Merger of Convergence, Divergence, and Salient Observations: An opportunity to change the culture and improve police-community relations. At the merger of the convergence and divergence of themes, as well as the salient

---

[22] R. T. Rybak, 2020. I was mayor of Minneapolis: I know why police reform fails. *The Atlantic.*

[23] Jill McCorkel, 2020. Police unions are one of the biggest obstacles to transforming policing. *The Conversation.*

observations, lie obstacles and an opportunity to change the culture and improve relational policing. Some elite interviewees offered suggestions to improve the relationship.

> We should begin promoting ourselves as "PEACE" officers, as opposed to law enforcement officers. Our daily missions should be to obtain peace regardless of the type of call we are responding to. We need to rebrand what we do and get away from the "warrior" and "meat eater" mentality.
>
> – Sheryl Victorian, African American female police professional

> The greatest opportunity is in this moment of unity when our country knows there is a mandate right now for change . . . community dialogues . . . that are occurring and that are proposed to bring all groups together to listen, to think, and to find a common ground for change.
>
> – Gail Milligan, white female community member

> Working with researchers and community members is paramount in trust and legitimacy. If change is imposed without the community's voice, there will be no moving forward. If researchers are not involved, there is no way to know if an initiative is effective or not.
>
> – Obed Magny, black male community member

> Dialogue without preconceptions of each other and prejudice. Both parties need to have willingness to listen and try to understand history's impact on other parties.
>
> – Yong Bacon, Korean American female police professional

To address the problems of a culture that is reinforced by the themes and salient observations, a few of the elite informants saw the need for additional research.

> Evidence and research confirm that widespread disparity exists in traffic stops and arrests, as well as victimization and access to resources that factor into social determinants of health and safety. We don't know exactly what changes are needed until we conduct more analysis to identify the sources of bias. America has an army of policing and social science researchers to employ in this endeavor. We should approach this epidemic as we are approaching COVID-19. Every possible option for investigation should be funded and promising practices should be accelerated.
>
> – Wendy Stivers, white female retired police professional

> Change is always good, but not if it is for the sake of change. When possible, change should come as a result of a body of research (not relying on what one study shows as all research has limitations). When immediate change is needed, attempts should be made to measure its effect under the principles of evidence-based policing.
>
> – Stephen Bishopp, white male police professional

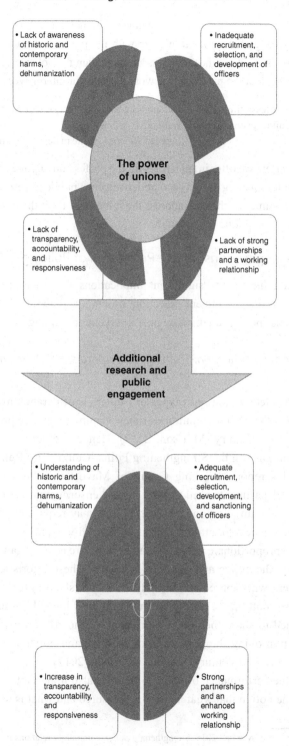

Figure 15 Alignment

Figure 15 provides a visual representation of how additional research, coupled with taking advantage of opportunities to engage with the public in meaningful and intentional ways, can address the cultural issues and align the policing profession with the expectations of the public. In the words of one our interviewees:

> The police profession may have dishonorable roots, but it can still bear the righteous fruit of justice, service, and unity.
> – Luke Bonkiewicz, white male police officer

In the next section, we offer implications for the profession of policing, future research, the policy-making process and police reforms, public governance, and postsecondary institutions that can address the issues that lie at the intersection of race, policing, and public governance.

4.2 Implications for the Profession of Policing

Our findings highlight some significant implications for the profession of policing related to the recruitment, selection, training, and appraisal of police officers. We focus specific attention on peer intervention training.

4.2.1 Recruitment, Selection, Training, and Appraisal of Performance of Officers

Recruiting and selecting the right types of officers is of paramount importance considering the current tumultuous times shaping the police profession for the twenty-first century (Morison, 2017). Hence, we echo the recommendations contained in the Strengthening Police-Community Relations in America's Cities report (Working Group of Mayors and Police Chiefs, 2015).[24] Police departments need to work toward ensuring that their officers are reflective of the jurisdictions they serve. This may require creative and innovative approaches to attract recruits, especially from communities impacted by disproportionate minority contacts that are often negative interactions between the police and minority residents. These efforts to recruit and hire officers who appreciate and have an understanding of disparate police services – both in the past and in the present – is vital. Officers like these are needed to share the values and vision of the community and are necessary for improving the profession of policing and police-community relations in twenty-first-century America (Morison, 2017).

Appraising the performance of police officers is also important. This calls into question the notion that what matters is measured and what is measured,

---

[24] The US Conference of Mayors, 2015. Strengthening police-community relations in America's cities.

matters. Scholars note that current police performance measures are inadequate and fail to capture many aspects of community-oriented policing (Williams et al., 2015; Rosenbaum et al., 2017). Consequently, more attention is needed to identify and measure community-oriented indicators of police performance as opposed to those traditional indicators that are more policing or institutional in nature (Williams, Brower & Klay, 2016). The traditional, standardized (one-size-fits-all) approach, which is common in local law enforcement departments across the United States, fails to meet community-centric needs that vary across jurisdictions. Findings from a study suggest the importance of tailoring appraisal forms and systems based upon job-specific rubrics and training modules that are informed by line and staff level officers (Williams et al., 2015). This bottom-up, top-down approach reflects a more expansive, yet insular approach to defining and appraising officer performance. To compliment this effort in a way that better reflects and aligns with the contemporary expectations of the community-oriented nature of policing requires the active involvement of community members in defining and appraising the performance of police officers. This involvement must be intentional, meaningful, and authentic in order to be impactful.

Recruiting and selecting the right types of officers is the initial step. Appraising the performance of officers is also necessary. But to better prepare officers to serve the diverse public of today in a fair, just, and equitable way requires mechanisms of exposure that allow officers to understand the history that comes with their badge and uniform. Lack of meaningful exposure to issues of race and disparate police treatment has been found to be missing in police and other related criminal justice textbooks (Turner, Giacopassi & Vandiver, 2006), therefore ill-equipping aspiring police professionals with a level of sensitivity and cultural competence that many segments of the American public now expect. Police aspirants both within the university setting and the academy need to be exposed to the role that police departments and their informal precursors have played in enforcing unjust and discriminatory laws and bigoted social norms – from the checking of travel passes during the days of slave patrols to the controversial contemporary policies and practices like stop and frisk – and the real impact of the use and abuse of these policies and practices on people of color as well as their perceptions (White & Fradella, 2016). Ignoring the past and neglecting the dystopian reality that lies at the juncture of race/ethnicity and policing (Walker & Brown, 1995) isn't feasible or expedient at the personal, professional, political, and societal levels.

Efforts are being made to expose more police officers to the biases that they have. Many departments and training academies are utilizing pre- and in-service training curriculum to alert officers to implicit bias as a way to mitigate the racial aspects of police shootings (Fridell, 2016). Fair and impartial policing is a curriculum that addresses disparate findings from some laboratory settings regarding shoot, don't shoot scenarios. In these sterile settings, law enforcement personnel, like other individuals, have been shown to associate black suspects more readily with weapons. But in these same settings, police officers have been found to be more hesitant to shoot black suspects when compared to whites (James et al., 2016). These findings are both bitter and sweet and call for additional research that will provide opportunities for new approaches to training to emerge.

Peer Intervention Training. A new approach to training police officers is emerging, and following the death of George Floyd it is gaining in relevancy. This type of training is called peer intervention training. As defined by Barbara Attard (2015) for the National Association for Civilian Oversight of Law Enforcement:

> Police Peer Intervention is a training program that teaches, in a practical and positive way, the powerful influence that police officers have on the conduct and behavior of their fellow officers. The training equips, encourages, and supports officers to intervene and prevent their colleagues from committing acts of serious misconduct and criminal behavior, particularly those directed against citizens. (Attard, 2015, p. 3)

The training can include education on the necessity of peer intervention, encouraging active bystandership, responsible whistleblowing, and ethical lessons on proper conduct (Aronie & Lopez, 2017; Bradley & MacIntyre, 2017).

Three truths form the core of why peer intervention was developed: (1) there are several common inhibitors to bystander intervention in any context, (2) the actions of others, or lack thereof, strongly impact the likelihood of others to intervene, and (3) the aggressor takes bystanders' inaction as acceptance or even support, and failure to intervene likely sets that as the pattern "inaction by others begets further inaction" (Aronie & Lopez, 2017: 298–99). If these three truths are addressed properly through the development, training, and education of officers, police peer intervention has a strong chance of succeeding. An influential work in the development of peer intervention training is *Walking with the Devil: The Police Code of Silence* by Mike Quinn (Attard, 2015; Aronie & Lopez, 2017). Quinn writes, "[t]his hate doesn't just stem from seeing bad cops do bad acts. More than anything, it grows out of the community's frustration with the good cops who do nothing to stop it" (Aronie & Lopez, 2017: 309). The development of peer intervention, therefore, can serve not only to prevent serious misconduct but also to mend the relationship between the police and the community.

Within police departments peer intervention training is still a relatively new concept. "While certainly there always have been and likely always will be officers who intervene in another's actions to prevent or mitigate misconduct or mistakes, the tools officers need to do so consistently, effectively, and safely rarely are taught in police academies" (Aronie & Lopez, 2017: 297). One department that has implemented a successful program is the New Orleans Police Department, a front-runner who received lots of attention for its ground-breaking efforts (Aronie & Lopez, 2017; Vasilogambros, 2020). Police departments that wish to implement a peer intervention training program would do well to use the New Orleans PD as a template. Additionally, peer intervention training programs exist in other professional fields, such as the military, medicine, and aviation among others (Aronie & Lopez, 2017; Bradley & MacIntyre, 2017; Vasilogambros, 2020).

For successful implementation, police peer intervention training programs must integrate diverse members of the police and the community, such as police officers and supervisors, civil rights lawyers, and community activists (Attard, 2015; Aronie & Lopez, 2017). Organizations must then conduct a series of dynamic training sessions during which the participants are educated on the importance of peer intervention training, and common myths about the training are debunked. Effective training methods are role-play scenarios, multimedia teaching, and an overall straightforward approach (Aronie & Lopez, 2017). Instead of focusing on the bad actors, peer intervention training targets those with the power to intervene through active bystandership (Attard, 2015; Aronie & Lopez, 2017; Vasilogambros, 2020). With a successful peer intervention training program, police officers are better equipped to protect the communities they serve and bring peace between the police and community members through transparency and trust.

Intentional effort to recruit, select, train, or develop and appraise the performance of police officers is needed. Including members of the public with police professionals in this process can meet the expectations of the public and propel American policing from its twentieth-century procedural policing model based upon policies and practices that were often discriminatory in nature to more of a twenty-first-century model of procedural policing (Bradford, 2014). This proposed model, which is based upon the procedural justice values of fairness and empowerment that promote organizational change and stronger relationships and partnerships between the public and the police, may play an important role and ultimately impact public support for policing in a positive way (Sunshine & Tyler, 2003).

4.3 Implications for Future Research

Research serves the purpose of gathering data that is used to explore, describe, and explain phenomena. Here, we offer implications for future research on representative bureaucracy, network sciences, and cocreation and coproduction that will serve the purpose of better understanding and addressing issues that lie at the intersection of race, policing, and public governance.

4.3.1 Representative Bureaucracy

Unlike the clear positive results of research on gender representation in police departments (Riccucci et al., 2014; Schuck, 2018), research on representative bureaucracy and race has resulted in contradicting findings. Some studies show an improvement in police-community relations and less frequent racial profiling with increased representation (Riccucci et al., 2018; Baumgartner et al., 2021), while others found the opposite to be true (Wilkins & Williams, 2008, 2009; Nicholson-Crotty, 2017). It has been hypothesized that this could be the result of intense organizational socialization, causing officers to identify more with the police force than civilian members of their own race. These inconsistencies prove the importance of future studies to better understand why representative bureaucracy can be more complex than it initially appears. Some suggestions for future research are as follows:

1. How do traffic stops and fruitless searches impact civic engagement and cooperation with police?
2. What are the costs and benefits of representative bureaucracy for police goals, and how to find a balance?
3. How does representation affect branches of an organization that are not race or gender specific?
4. How does race affect the social aspects of police culture?
5. How does the partnering of officers, officer gender, and officer seniority affect the results of representation?

Additionally, future research should consider continuing some of the existing studies on representational bureaucracy in more detail or in different real-world settings. Another common point is that future research should investigate *why* these findings exist, not simply questioning their existence. More specifically, for studies on the representation of a specific group, especially when related to an important social concern, there should be further examination of the findings and what other influences could affect the results. For example, do Latino officers actually profile Latino citizens or does their presence cause other officers to act differently? Addressing these points in future research will increase the validity of experiments on representational bureaucracy and improve the trustworthiness of their findings. Once representation is better understood, it will be easier to see how representative bureaucracy can be used to improve the relationship between police officers and the community they serve.

4.3.2 Networks Sciences

Research on networks in policing has painted a clear picture of their critical importance to policing and police culture. A network position study in Chicago indicated that although only a small percentage of Chicago Police Department (CPD) officers shoot, those officers who do occupy the unique position within police networks of being a network broker and connecting otherwise disparate sections of the greater police network (Zhao & Papachristos, 2020). These findings mean that if these officers who are network brokers are more likely to shoot, then policies should be focused on ways to prevent them from occupying this key position and then intervening when they do. Knowledge of these findings now makes it insufficient to only account for individual demographic risk factors. Police departments must begin to understand and take a closer look at their officers within the broader context of their police social networks. This has implications for additional research. Future studies should explore:

1. What are the specific informal network settings where officers are socialized, and what are the mechanisms by which it occurs?
2. How can police departments better influence informal social networks to promote an atmosphere of positive accountability? What is traditionally thought to be effective versus what is actually effective?
3. Outside of rank and formal organizationally given sources of power, who are the officers within the department with the most influence?
4. What are the ways in which officers with informal and nontraditional sources of power and influence come to occupy these positions?
5. How are officers with informal positions of power using these positions to promote cultures of accountability and compliance or cultures of deviance and misconduct?

> Police social networks and corresponding positioning within them have significant impact not only on policing in general, but specifically on police culture and use of force. These networks effectively dictate what behaviors are acceptable and which are not. Furthermore, these implications impact the blue code of silence and which behaviors are acceptable to be reported and which are not (Klockars et al., 2000). With this knowledge of the power of networks and network positioning, it now becomes of paramount importance to engage in additional inquiry, particularly devoted to investigating how to positively influence these networks so that coinciding behaviors can also be positively

influenced down the line. Findings from these and related studies can result in establishing new norms that push deviant behavior further into what is abnormal and bring accountability back into the norm. Using knowledge of police networks from future studies presents an opportunity to intervene early, change culture, and ultimately prevent the unnecessary loss of life.

4.3.3 Cocreation and Coproduction

Cocreation and coproduction have been shown to improve police community relations by including all voices and creating and implementing policy through collaboration and innovation. Despite the research that has been conducted regarding cocreation and coproduction, there are gaps that remain to be investigated. Future research should mimic previous studies, testing their validity and including different populations and concerns. The various factors discovered that influence coproduction should be more clearly defined and the coproduction process must be better managed. Williams et al. (2016), Uzochukwu and Thomas (2018) and Dudau et al. (2019) call for future studies to continue their work and to go more in-depth into the investigation of their theories and the results that follow. It is imperative that future research recognizes the relationship between different factors that influence coproduction. Without gaining this understanding it will be impossible to state a single cause of any behavior toward or against coproduction. Future research should consider exploring the following:

1. What are some ways the effectiveness of cocreation and coproduction can be improved?
2. How can citizens and police cocreate future experiments?
3. Will other studies involving vulnerable or marginalized populations produce the same results?
4. How does an individual's identity and demographics affect their relationship with police and cocreation and coproduction behavior?
5. What can increase community participation in cocreation and coproduction?

Brandsen et al. (2018) offer additional practical recommendations for future research. They suggest that the potentials of cocreation and coproduction justify future experimentation on the topics but that differences in public administration should be considered and expectations should be tempered. Service providers and citizens should be involved in experiment creation, incentives should be tailored to each citizen group, digital options should be developed, and cocreation and coproduction experiments should be paired with specialized training strategies for professionals for experimental success (Brandsen et al., 2018). If these suggestions are followed and future research continues to attempt to improve the effectiveness and reliability of cocreation and coproduction programs, this collaboration between police and community members will be an invaluable step forward to the future.

4.4 Implications for Public Policy-Making Process and Police Reform

Practical implications abound relative to the focal topic of this Element. There are numerous opportunities to revise the process for public policy making and additional considerations for police reform. However, we limit our discussion to three areas that could have a positive impact on police-community relations on the other side of now. Those areas are reimagining and redesigning police policies and practices, reexamining the reasonableness standard in the *Graham* decision, and reconsidering the doctrine of qualified immunity.

4.4.1 Reimagining and Redesigning Police Policies

To reimagine means to reconceive, to reconsider. To maximize the impact and effectiveness of reimagining, it has to be inclusive, especially when considering the need to better redesign police policies, programs, and practices from lenses of equity, diversity, and inclusion.

The findings from our data illuminated the opportunity to couple police with community residents in reimagining and redesigning the policies and related practices for police departments and their officers. But, with this opportunity come obstacles that were reflected in many of the quotes. Overcoming the obstacles of lack of trust and understanding are opportunities for police-community listening and learning exchanges. These settings allow for participants to share their respective lived experiences that impact, shape, and inform their worldview or perspective as well as to hear and hopefully understand, but not necessarily agree with, the perspectives of others when they share their lived experiences. This process achieves the goal of a true dialogue – to speak across differences.

Our findings encourage local communities to take advantage of the opportunity to be more inclusive in securing the participation of stakeholders to reenvision, redesign, and restructure or reorganize police policies, practices, programs/services, and structures. Obstacles are present, but the potential rewards in engaging in this effort outweigh the risks.

4.4.2 A Reexamination of the Reasonableness Standard: What Is Reasonableness?

In *Graham* (1989), determining whether the force used is "reasonable" under the Fourth Amendment requires a careful balancing or the "nature and quality of the intrusion on the individual's Fourth Amendment interest" against the countervailing governmental interests at stake. The test of reasonableness under the Fourth Amendment in our current legal system is not quite capable of a precise definition or mechanical application. To properly apply the reasonableness tests, courts must take a facts and circumstances approach while taking special interest in the severity of the crime, whether the suspect poses an immediate threat to the safety of the officers or others, and whether he is actively resisting arrest or attempting to evade arrest by flight (Brown, 1991). The question is "whether the totality of the circumstance justifies a particular sort of . . . seizure" to determine the constitutionality of the seizure (Shafer, 1982).

The reasonableness of a particular use of force must be judged from the perspective of a reasonable officer on the scene rather than with the 20/20 vision of hindsight. When analyzing excessive use of force claims, the reasonableness at the moment of the incident applies: "[N]ot every push or shove, even if it may later seem unnecessary in the peace of a judge's chambers" violates the Fourth Amendment (*Graham* v. *Connor*, 1989). When determining reasonableness, the Court must account for the fact that police officers are often forced to make split-second decisions – in circumstances that are tense, uncertain, and rapidly evolving – about the amount of force that is necessary in a particular situation (*Graham* v. *Connor*, 1989).

The reasonableness standard set forth in *Graham* is one of objective analysis and not one of subjective analysis. This is strikingly different from the subjective substantive due process standard used by Judge Friendly in *Glick*. The question is whether the officers' actions are "objectively reasonable" in light of the facts and circumstances confronting them without regard to their underlying intent or motivations. This means that an officer's evil intentions will not make a Fourth Amendment violation out of an objectively reasonable use of force nor will an officer's good intentions make an objectively unreasonable use of force constitutional.

***Glick* test versus reasonableness.** Judge Friendly in *Johnson v. Glick* (1973), the precursor to *Graham* v. *Connor* (1989), outlined four distinct factors to determine the constitutionality of police use of force. Instead of grounding the standard in the text of the Constitution, Judge Friendly looked to substantive due process. He held that "quite apart from any specific of Bill of Rights, application of undue force by law enforcement officers deprives a suspect of liberty without due process of the laws" (*Johnson v. Glick*, 1973). Judge Friendly reasoned that a correctional officer's use of similarly excessive force must give rise to a due process violation actionable under §1983 (*Johnson v. Glick*, 1973). Judge Friendly went on to set forth four factors to guide courts in determining "whether the constitutional line has been crossed" by a particular use of force (*Johnson v. Glick*, 1973). Initially, Friendly held that uses of force that "shocks the conscience" violates the Fourteenth Amendment" (*Johnson v. Glick*, 1973). He eventually established the "*Glick* test," a test that requires consideration of (1) the need for the application of force; (2) the relationship between the need and the amount of force that was used; (3) the extent of the injury inflicted; and (4) whether the force was applied in a "good faith effort to maintain and restore discipline or maliciously and sadistically for the very purpose of causing harm" (*Johnson v. Glick*, 1973). This standard accounts for the subjective intent of the arresting or detaining officer in order to warrant a constitutional violation.

In *Graham*, the Court essentially overturned *Glick* and as a result the *Glick* test by holding that "the Court of Appeals erred in analyzing it under the four-part *Glick* test" and that "the malicious and sadistic factor puts in issue the subjective motivation of the individual officers, which our prior cases make clear has no bearing on whether a particular seizure is 'unreasonable' under the Fourth Amendment" (*Graham* v. *Connor*, 1989). Instead the Court illustrated the fact-intensive reasonableness standard to govern excessive force claims under §1983. Although this new reasonableness standard eliminates the need for a subjective inquiry into the defendant's motive, the standard is increasingly deferential to police officers, making it increasingly more difficult to find their actions unreasonable under the circumstances (Schwartz, 2017).

Comparing standards? In evaluating the two standards that govern excessive use of force claims, differences occur when the subject of the analysis hinges on the subjective intent of the officer. When an officer exudes force without the proper intent or motivation, under the *Glick* standard, the plaintiff will likely win their suit. For example, in *Lewis* v. *Downs* (1985), the Court of Appeals for the Sixth Circuit used the *Glick* standard to determine the constitutionality of police use of force. In *Lewis* v. *Downs* (1985), two officers arrived at the Lewis home to respond to a noise complaint. During the response, both officers struck Mr. Lewis, Mrs. Lewis, and their son Tony, injuring them all (*Lewis* v. *Downs*, 1985). The court found in favor of the Lewis family, holding that the officers "acted maliciously in applying the force" (Lewis v. Downs, 1985). The court came to this conclusion by evaluating the necessity of force in relation to the threat of harm posed by the Lewis family. If this case were to be evaluated under the now-controlling reasonableness Fourth Amendment standard, it is likely that a court would also find use of force as objectively unreasonable.

The impact of the *Graham* decision is felt when the officer acts in a "good faith effort to maintain or restore discipline" but makes an objectively unreasonable decision about the degree of force used under the circumstances

(*Graham* v. *Connor*, 1989). When this happens, the plaintiff should win under the *Graham* reasonableness standard, but the defendant should win under the *Glick* standard because of the lack of improper intent. The *Graham* standard catches those cases of excessive use of force that may have been permissible under the *Glick* test solely due to the subjective intent of the officer. At first glance, it seems as though the reasonableness standard is more expansive and therefore more plaintiff friendly, but that is rarely the case in practice. Courts are deferential to governmental actors and therefore hesitant to find police action as unreasonable. Take the case *Jamieson* v. *Shaw* (1985), for example. In this case, the defendant police officers knowingly pulled behind a car driven by a mentally ill man in which the minor plaintiff was riding. Once the light switched to green, the minor accelerated and a police chase ensued. After the officers radioed for assistance from the state highway patrol, a roadblock was set up to capture the plaintiff. When the minor's car reached the roadblock, state highway patrol officers flashed a bright light in the plaintiff's eyes, causing him to subsequently lose control of the vehicle and crash. The minor suffered extensive injuries as a result of the police action. On appeal, the dissent highlighted the great deference given to police actions. Furthermore, the dissenting judge warned against "inappropriate second-guessing of police officers' split-second decisions" (*Jamieson* v. *Shaw*, 1985). If courts continue to show this sort of deference to clearly unreasonable police action, the *Graham* case does nothing to add to the legal framework of excessive use of force.

4.4.3 Implications for the Doctrine of Qualified Immunity

The implications of the qualified immunity defense are multifold. By raising this defense early in the trial process, police officers are shielded from the discovery process – the practice where both parties in privity of suit request and receive information needed to structure their respective cases. Under the defense of qualified immunity, if granted, plaintiffs are barred from accessing this information that could potentially be relevant in highlighting a persistent culture of police misconduct in a given district. Qualified immunity also protects police officers whose actions are seemingly excessive to the average citizen, so long as those officers have plausible deniability of the existence of the violation of the individual's civil liberties.

4.5 Implications for Pubic Governance: The Governance Challenge

With the growing diversity of American society, complications accompany our transition from the melting pot metaphor that encouraged assimilation toward the proverbial salad bowl where acceptance of difference is respected. This transition highlights a public governance challenge – the evolving role of the state and its residents engaging in a concerted fashion to improve the livelihoods of the public and well-being of the community (OECD, 2009) and the implications for sharing power and the distribution of responsibility to public servants and the public they serve.

4.5.1 Implications for Power with and a Shared Sense of Responsibility

Effective leadership is about creating a vision of a desired future state that compels others to assist in making that vision a reality. This attribute of leadership speaks to power – the ability to influence the actions of others.

Mary Parker Follett (1998) provided a conceptual understanding of what a "new state" would require and the needed power to make that new state a functioning reality. The new state would require leadership to utilize the principles of coordination that would foster and increase a sense of power among those being led. This approach would leverage a "power with" rather than a "power over" strategy to get things done. Leaders in this context would have to create more leaders. This leader producing, "power with" approach rested upon integration – a process that brought people together to reach a common goal or objective. In this context, the "others" were expected and encouraged to participate in this process because they could add value through their perspectives, and their contributions were vital and beneficial in achieving the goal. This integrated, "power with" approach advances the notion of a shared sense of responsibility where individuals working collaboratively can identify and solve the problems facing its society (Follett, 1998).

At the intersection of race, policing, and public governance lies an opportunity for the public and police to share power, responsibility, and leadership in a coordinated and distributed way by acknowledging the wicked problems of the past but, more importantly, to recognize and address those problems in the present and in the future. This collaborative approach to problem identification, problem understanding, and problem mitigation requires an empowering form of leadership, coupled with effective management that promotes group power over professional or individual power in the pursuit of what's good for the public (Follett, 1998). This approach has applications and implications for not only communities and organizations but also postsecondary institutions.

4.6 Implications for Postsecondary Institutions

Around us is a world polarized, filled with hate and injustice. Through racism, displacement, violence, and famine, it is clear that our world is broken.

However, through faith and belief in the inherent goodness of human nature, this situation is not a death sentence but an opportunity for action – action that has implications for postsecondary institutions.

4.6.1 Student Learning

Institutions of higher education pride themselves in being centers of knowledge cultivation where students are prepared and leaders are created to go into the world to be both good and great. To make a difference. To add voice and value to the dialogue – the speaking across differences – around race, policing, and public governance. University students have a unique role in this conversation. They are the next generation of policy makers, professionals, politicians, educators, and activists. They have the ability to help shape how our world will look. They have the power to change our world – our policies, programs, and professional practices.

Despite this, graduates of universities across the nation are too often entering the world with a gaping hole in their preparation as a result of never being significantly exposed to issues of race, equity, and how they affect aspects of everyday life such as policing and public governance more broadly. In an ever-diversifying world, and in the political climate of today, there is simply no way for one to truly be a competent leader without an in-depth and nuanced understanding of such topics. This matter becomes even more important when coupled with the ability of many college students, namely white students, to grow up in a white community, go. to white schools, attend a white university, work for a white company, and repeat this cycle of never meaningfully interacting with topics of race and equity with their next generation. Universities can and should disrupt this cycle. If preparing students and developing leaders is going to remain a priority for universities across the United States, they are obligated to do more to ensure that students leave their campuses culturally competent and with a firm handle on the issues and implications of race and equity.

So, what are the implications of this problem for student learning? We provided some examples for your consideration.

Mandated course on race and equity. The most impactful measure that could be implemented to ensure this understanding is gained is to develop and mandate an engaging course on race and equity to be incorporated into all students' curriculum. This proposal will undoubtedly face opposition. Critics will say universities are taking a political stance, overlooking that such a course will be fact-driven and historical in nature, presenting an additional opportunity to teach students how to interpret histories and facts for themselves. Critics will also say that there is no room for such a course, ignoring the fact that many universities already have curricula that mandate credits in areas such as the natural sciences, mathematics, and languages, even for students who have no stated interest in those fields. Along the same lines, critics will point out that a mandatory course on race and equity is not pertinent to some students' field of study or desired career. A critique of this sort demonstrates exactly why such a course is needed. Though students may not have a stated interest in learning about issues of race and equity, everyone is implicated and involved in these systems one way or another. Whether it is pre-health students learning about the harmful legacy of eugenics and social determinants of health or public policy students learning about housing discrimination and systemic voter discrimination, every area of study, like every area of life, is affected by issues of race and equity. Universities can and should be flexible with such a course, and these things will be imperative when navigating the critiques that will arise. Though implementation of such a course would be challenging, rather than seeing it as an obstacle to overcome, universities should see this as an opportunity to fulfill their missions of preparing students and creating leaders to be both great and good.

Assignments to appreciate the other.   The crux of the issue is that people do not understand each other. Once we open our minds to other opinions and acknowledge each of our unique lived experiences, we will have more respect for the other side, even when we still disagree. How we are raised shapes how we think. There is nothing wrong with being affected by your circumstances, but we must each realize that no one else's circumstances will have been the same as ours and therefore other people will think differently. Our minds must be open to other possibilities. Students need to be taught to approach people with different backgrounds and opinions by learning about them and respecting their beliefs, thereby acknowledging the humanity of others. To feel hate toward a group may be easy; it is more difficult to hate an individual that you have come to know and understand. Learning more about the story and beliefs of an individual member of a group helps bridge the gap between people who would seem to be very different and softens the hate and prejudice against other members of the group, be that race, nationality, or religion.

Accomplishing the acknowledgment, acceptance, and respect for differences requires direct action in the form of a learning exchange. We propose a two-part model, completed over one to two class periods during the semester of an already-required course. This in-class model could additionally be supplemented by assigned reading of differing yet respectfully presented opinions on various topics. The first portion of this exchange would be of an introspective nature: Students would be asked a series of prewritten questions on their beliefs about certain topics, such as,

1. Where and how were you raised? (country/state, rural/urban, family beliefs)
2. How would you describe your relationship to law enforcement in your community?
3. Have you experienced racism or prejudice in any capacity? If so, what is an example?
4. What are your beliefs regarding religion and political affiliation?

After writing responses to these questions, students would then be asked to reflect on why they hold their beliefs and how their backgrounds may have shaped their responses. The goal of this first portion of the exchange would be to encourage students to think about how lived experiences shape opinions and that no one point of view is absolute.

The second portion of the learning experience would consist of students sharing their responses with another student in class with a different background. Students should be encouraged to share all opinions, especially when they differ from their classmates. The pair of students would then write a brief reflection on what beliefs and experiences they share and where they differ, including an analysis of how each of their lived experiences shaped these similarities and differences. This exercise will help humanize members of groups a student may not regularly interact with (such as students of a different race or nationality) and will decrease the likelihood of future stereotyping, prejudice, and intolerance. Ideally, students' future approach to viewing opposing beliefs will be inquisitive with the aim of understanding how the beliefs were formed and approach differences with open-mindedness and a desire to learn.

Implications for legal studies. From a law school perspective, much can be accomplished to redress the inequities that plague § 1983 suits. Law students are positioned to elicit change in the way the reasonableness standard is applied. By lobbying for clear police protocols that establish baseline "reasonable" measures by police to "seize" a citizen, these students can offer the court a more cut-and-dry case for unreasonability. Lobbying for policies banning inappropriate knee-on-neck procedures and limitations for physical force would likely translate to a ruling of unreasonable behavior by the court. Because reasonableness as gauged by the court is reflected by the ordinary, sensible police officer, law students can assist in efforts to bring clarity and uniformity in use of force protocol that can serve as the needed baseline for reasonable police behavior.

4.6.2 Student Engagement

Universities, many of them with racist histories including racist founders, need to begin reckoning with their pasts. They are often home to aloof students who stroll through campus with no real historical understanding of how their university became what it is today. As students play on lawns and landscapes shaped by enslaved laborers or walk under statues exalting men they should abhor, frequently an air of suspicion intertwines with a light breeze of guilt, but too often students are simply too afraid or too apathetic to go the next step and learn of the atrocities that occurred to build the place they call home. For this reason, they make an unconscious or sometimes explicitly conscious decision to remain ignorant.

Though students may be hesitant to take this next step, universities can assist students in this growth process with education on their histories that center on the black and brown people whose pain and unpaid sacrifices made their universities a reality. This type of education can be initially implemented at first student contact during first-year orientations and renewed annually through online forums. Furthermore, many institutions have historical tours, but they remain widely unattended by the students who attend the school. Universities should consider ways to publicize and incentivize students to go on these learning expeditions. There is no acceptable reason why these valuable historical tours and educational opportunities should not be promoted alongside other programs that encourage school spirit and student engagement. They are equally, if not more, important.

To complement this effort, university students have a responsibility to form a positive relationship with both the community in which their university resides and the police officers who serve the university and broader community. Universities have a tremendous impact on the livelihoods of the surrounding community. Due to this fact and because the majority of students do not permanently reside in the community surrounding their university, students should consider themselves long-term guests and partners of the community. The same is true with law enforcement officers who work at the university and beyond its campus. As it is the officers' duty to protect and serve the public, this relationship should be an amicable partnership instead of one characterized by antagonistic suspicion. Provided that police departments make necessary changes as explained in prior sections, the university students' role should be one of partnership working toward the common good.

We propose that this positive relationship be spearheaded by a student governance committee, modeled after the University of Virginia's approach to student governance and the honor system. Universities should implement a student committee with two primary roles: engaging with the community and engaging with law enforcement. These committees will have regular meetings with police officers, supervisors, business owners, and employees who work alongside the university. The meetings would consist of a discussion of issues that arise, concerns, and potential solutions. All members should have an opportunity to share their voice and the goal should be to listen and strategize together to arrive at an answer. Students should be chosen through interest and selection, as those students with the greatest desire to participate will likely be those with the most knowledge surrounding the issues at hand. The university students who participate in these governance committees must first be trained in contemporary social concerns and educated on what research has shown to be effective and ineffective solutions. A consistent dialogue between university students, community members, and law enforcement officers will help the police better understand and address students' concerns and will help students learn how to best engage responsibly with the community.

4.6.3 Student Advocacy and Action

On college campuses across the nation, student advocacy groups are hosting necessary conversations around race, policing, and issues of equity. Advocacy is one of the strongest powers for change, as sometimes all it takes is one voice to spark change across a nation. From Mahatma Gandhi's peaceful yet powerful resistance in India and South Africa to Rosa Parks' brave defiance spearheading the civil rights movement in the United States, to the graffiti of young boys that started the Syrian revolution, it is clear that the voice of one can inspire the actions of many. The Black Lives Matter movement is a contemporary advocacy success story, inspiring a nation and beyond and creating real change, but advocacy should not stop here.

We encourage students to take action for the causes that they believe in, whatever that may be. Some opportunities may be presented as clubs and organizations affiliated with the university or, if none are available, students can pioneer a new advocacy club. Student organizations are holding discussions to build bridges, some even naming themselves such, like the University of Virginia's BRIDGE (Bringing Race into Dialogue with Group Engagement), with the stated vision of a university community that is welcoming and inclusive to all those who are in it. In addition to these student groups, across the country Black Student Alliances and Black Student Unions are organizing to lobby their school's administration to enact desperately needed change.

Perhaps there is a job opportunity or volunteer work available that is involved with policing or the local community. Maybe a role in the student council or a student governance committee will serve as the stepping-stone to create university-wide policy change. Other students may choose to share their beliefs with people they are close to and to encourage others to join the cause alongside them. The continuous development of digital networks and social media presents another avenue for students to share their voice and become advocates. It is clear that many options are available for students to take a stand and capitalize on the platform their university offers. However, no one should dictate how someone else advocates for their cause. That is an inherently personal decision and one we encourage all students to consider. Students can ask themselves these questions: What do I believe is worth taking a stand for? How can I best take action? Why does it matter to me?

Like undergraduate students, law students have the opportunity and unique ability to serve clients seeking to file § 1983 suits against governmental officials. Clinics within law schools provide students with opportunities to learn practical legal skills by working with clients. By creating a civil rights litigation clinic, law schools across the country can facilitate the influx of cases to challenge the standing reasonableness standard as it applied to § 1983 suits. Students working with plaintiffs may earn pro bono hours as a result of their assistance with the preliminary steps necessary to initiate a suit.

Undergraduate, graduate, and professional students are tired of the social injustices and inequities. At this moment in time, students are initiating and leading emotionally taxing conversations about race, petitioning their administration for change, attending day-long protests for George Floyd and Breonna Taylor – and are expected to show up to class on Monday ready to learn. Dating back to Ruby Bridges having tomatoes thrown at her for having the audacity to attend elementary school, students of color, namely black students, must face similar challenges as they attempt to not only survive, but to thrive at predominantly white schools in a predominantly white nation. Black students are tired, resulting not only from these challenges but from the lack of meaningful support from university leadership and their white classmates. The diversity of protest crowds at marches for George Floyd and Breonna Taylor has been promising, but in the classroom all too often white students sit silently when racially insensitive comments are made that make their black classmates feel uncomfortable. That silence is arguably just as harmful. Black students continue to fight, advocate, use their voices, spend their time, show up to class, study, work, and more. They do this all for the chance to someday be able to be free and unbothered – for the chance to be able to focus solely on academics and living out what many hoped to be some of the best years of their life. However, we are not there yet, so still they fight. And in the classic fashion of black people across the United States and across the world, they have harkened to the inspiring words of Maya Angelou[25] and like dust, still they rise.

---

[25] Maya Angelou, 1978. "And Still I Rise."

4.6.4 The Evolving Role of Postsecondary Institutions

Washing one's hands of the conflict between the powerful and the powerless means to side with the powerful, not to be neutral.

– Paulo Freire

Postsecondary education in the United States is a continuation of study after high school. Its purpose is to equip students with the needed knowledge, skills, and abilities to pursue a specific career. The traditional role of higher education institutions is to support and improve the quality of life of American society. Postsecondary institutions accrue benefits at the individual and collective levels; they build and deepen human capital (Abel & Deitz, 2011). This process has been done with an emphasis on teaching, research, service, and engagement. These focal areas have led to universities and colleges being described as citizens who promote leadership, service, and democracy (Bringle, Games & Malloy, 1999).

Postsecondary institutions, like all institutions, continue to evolve and grow based upon their ecosystems. These institutions are described as incubators and facilitators for desegregating American society (Milem, Umbach, & Liang, 2004); learning laboratories that explore, discuss, and encourage liberation (Manning, 1994); and as educational settings for critical consciousness (Freire, 1989). Within the classrooms, lecture halls, student centers, and amphitheaters on campuses across the United States, students are exposed to diverse information, often in the context of historic harms that have surfaced in areas plagued by racial violence or, in the words of Ward (2016), "microclimates of racial meaning." Exposure to new information provides a deeper understanding of the past and its impact on the present and challenges preconceived notions. This exposure generates the needed cultural capital and cultural connectedness to mend the tear in the social fabric of American society and encourages advocacy and action (Davis, 1998).

On the other side of now, postsecondary institutions must accept the charge that their evolving role demands. Through their teaching, research, service, and engagement, they must embrace an expanding but necessary role of advancing citizenship, equity, and social justice in the twenty-first century (Harkavy, 2006). A clarion call to advocacy and action in fields and disciplines within postsecondary institutions has been voiced (Marsiglia & Williams, 2011; Benfer, 2015; Blessett et al., 2019). Now continues to be the time for those within the academic halls of postsecondary institutions and beyond to heed those calls, even if it results in "good" and "necessary trouble." Higher education institutions are institutions of advocacy and action. They should embrace the timeless words of John Lewis.

Do not get lost in a sea of despair. Be hopeful, be optimistic. Our struggle is not the struggle of the day, a week, a month, or a year, it is the struggle of a lifetime. Never, ever be afraid to make some noise and get in good trouble, necessary trouble.

5 Conclusion

In the worst of times, incredibly, that's when hope appears, like a seed, like a bulb splitting. One never knows what it costs a bulb to split, a lily bulb or an onion, to split open. And that tendril to come out ... there's a song in Genesis, there's a statement that it had rained so long, that people had given up the idea that rain would cease. And then the Lord said that He would put a rainbow in the sky ... Now that means that in the worst of times, in the dreariest of times, you can look right into the clouds and see hope.

– Maya Angelou (West, 1999: 189)

Jason Isbell [26] asked a very striking question: How do we get white people living in a white man's world to appreciate the different, disparate, and often dystopian world of black and brown people? This is especially salient in the context of police interactions.

How can hope be restored at the intersection of past and present, where the wreckage from the collision of race and policing is still present? This Element, much like Cornel West's (1999) *Restoring Hope: Conversations on the Future of Black America*, provides some informed insights. It has highlighted the obstacles and opportunities to deconstruct the dystopian policies, programs, practices, and structures of the past and has encouraged processes that reimagine, redesign, and reconstruct policies, practices, programs, and structures that can form a more perfect union. In essence, our Element urges getting to the first word of the Preamble of the US Constitution: we.

Together we can form a more perfect union. Together we can bridge the gaps that divide and mend the frays of our social fabric. Together we can out of many, become one. Together we can issue and respond to a clarion call to action. Together we can have a better reality on the other side of now. But it will come with a cost.

It has been said that where your treasure is, there your heart will be also. We must make an investment of capital: financial, social, cultural, emotional, and intellectual to begin the process of becoming aware, understanding, acknowledging, and engaging in collective compassionate action. More research is needed to serve as a probing light that brings awareness of what has occurred and what is occurring. This light can guide our efforts to take

---

[26] Jason Isbell and the 400 Unit, 2017. "White Man's World."

a coactive approach much like the city of Richmond, Virginia[27] – one that couples the police with the public that it serves – to reimagine and redesign public safety from a human services lens, to address excessive use of force, and to leverage community engagement to bring about healing and community wholeness.

We are facing a FUBU moment – a time where we discuss, design, and implement policies, programs, and professional practices in the context of policing that are FUBU – for us, by us. The us referred to here is a collective, inclusive us, an us that reflects the diversity of thought, race, ethnicity, orientation, religion, disciplinary leanings, and political ideologies of US. We can learn from the CAHOOTS (Crisis Assistance Helping out on the Streets) model in Eugene, Oregon, that reimagined and redesigned policing and public safety where social workers and police professionals now share responsibility in serving those in need.

Like in Eugene, what resides at the other side of race, policing, and public governance is dependent upon the individual and collective us. We are free to engage in collective action to understand and address the historical and ongoing problems of race and policing. We also have the freedom to not engage. But, we shall be free[28] when this issue and others like unemployment and underemployment, affordable housing, poverty, hunger, access to quality health care, food deserts, all part and parcel of systemic racism are addressed – collectively.

It has been said that mourning comes at the midnight hour. This statement is true, but a similar statement is equally true. Morning comes at the midnight hour as well. It depends upon the "u" at the individual level, the "u" in the US, and in us at the national and global levels. A new day does emerge after each night. New opportunities to learn from the mistakes of yesterday come with each day. To grow. To evolve. To right wrongs. This appreciation for the irony of life causes us to recall and revise the song of Aretha Franklin[29] – that this temporary darkness will never break our faith in a brighter tomorrow.

The Book of Ecclesiastes, the third chapter and the first verse, reminds its readers of seasons, times, and purposes. We have witnessed a time to die, a time to kill, a time to weep, a time to mourn, a time of silence, a time of distancing, a time to lose, a time to rend, and a time of hate. Now is the time to plant, to heal, to build up, to embrace, to keep, to mend, to speak, and to love. Now is the time for awareness, understanding, acknowledgment, and for individual and collective compassionate action. Now is the time for innovative research. Now is the

---

[27] WRIC Newsroom, 2020. Mayor Stoney presents: Task force for reimagining public safety.
[28] Garth Brooks, 1992. "We Shall Be Free."
[29] Aretha Franklin and The Boys Choir of Harlem, 2006. "Never Gonna Break My Faith."

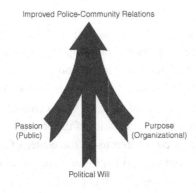

Figure 16 Improved police-community relations.

time to couple state and lay actors. Now is the time for progressive policies, programs, and professional practices that have been codesigned and cocreated. Now is the time for peace that must be coproduced. We are at the convergence of change where public passion, political will, and institutional and organizational purpose can come together due to a greater awareness, understanding, acknowledgment, and compassionate action to improve police-community relations (see Figure 16). One day, the war will be won. One day, the glory will come. Glory![30] This is the vision for the other side of now.

5.1 Our Final Thoughts: A Matter of the Heart

Only when it is dark enough . . . can you see the stars.
– Martin Luther King, Jr.

BLM – Black Lives Matter. The present-day visceral reaction that some people have to those three letters is similar to the same type of reaction during the civil rights era to the letters SNCC – the Student Nonviolent Coordinating Committee – or NAACP – the National Association for the Advancement of Colored People. It seems that the past continues to have a presence in the present. But can tomorrow be different? Can it be brighter and better?

Laura Coates recently offered an insight that was spot-on. She noted that people mattering, much like justice, isn't a pie with only a limited number of slices . . . where if one group gets their slice of mattering, justice, or respect for

---

[30] Common and John Legend, 2014. "Glory."

their humanity that others will automatically get less. She was persuasive. This zero-sum game way of thinking must be challenged as we are reminded once again of the problems that accompany this philosophy.

Addressing the problem that lies at the intersection of race and policing in America requires a clean heart in order to create within its body politic the right type of spirit, resolve, and strength to take on this seemingly never-ending Sisyphean task. This task ultimately is a matter of the heart.

The heart is important. It is considered to be the center of our being. The impact of a clean, well-functioning heart isn't limited or contained to just that organ. The heart empowers other organs. It functions as the pumping station to vital portions of our body. The heart supplies all of our organs with blood. The blood, our life source, travels throughout our entire body and impacts our head, our ears, our eyes, our mouth, our hands, and our feet. A clean heart that functions properly shows evidence.

With a clean heart, we should have a new mind. We should think new thoughts, have new ideas. Within the academic environment, we should think about research and research questions differently.

With a clean heart, we should strive to listen more and to speak less. This will allow us to understand, value, and respect the lived experiences of others whose lives may be much different than our own.

With a clean heart, we should find creative and innovative ways to look at people, places, spaces, and other data points differently. This may allow us to get a clearer view of how the historic harms of the past impact the present.

With a clean heart, we should speak differently. We should advocate based upon a fresh awareness of the challenges of achieving equity, social justice, diversity, and inclusion by sharing our understanding of the disparate, dystopian, and disheartening interconnectedness of outcomes across policy domains. We must speak truth and we must speak truth to power. We have to understand that the power of life and death can be in our tongues. But as we speak or advocate, we must accept the challenge of Ralph Waldo Emerson – that our actions must speak so loudly that no one can hear what we are saying.

Our actions are in our hands. As scholars, our hands play a vital role in what we research and write – what we do and produce for others.

Our actions are also in our feet. We need our feet to go to those places and spaces in order to understand and assist others. The actions that flow from our hearts, to our minds, eyes, ears, mouths, hands, and feet should be centered on others and not on ourselves.

We have an opportunity to engage in life-changing and life-saving work. This work is beyond being important – the type of work that is self-centered. The work we must engage in is significant – it is all about others. Its significance is reflected in the urgency of now. How long can we wait?

How Long?
by Domenick E. Bailey

How long can I stay patient when innocent lives are lost faster than I can write these words?
How long can dreams of justice and equality continue to be deferred?

How long can you stay silent and complicit?
How long until white folks learn to sit down and listen?
How long until we get meaningful policies?
How long until they're not created in rooms where not a soul looks like me?

How long until we do more than change the street signs?
(Black Lives Matter Plaza is nice, but how about addressing those redlines?)

How long until talk and action finally meet?
How long until officers are willing to see my humanity?

How long until social justice is no longer trending?
How long until the language of the unheard is re-spoken, because they still aren't comprehending?

How long until the pain goes away?
How long until we can see that promised, brighter day?

How long until we're no longer on the run?
How long until Black mothers can stop pushing to the back of their minds –

How long until it's my son?

As we think about the current state of police-community relations and the opportunity to mitigate the problems embedded within, we know that we must act now. This is a matter of our hearts because our hearts affect our total being.

Where your heart is, that is where your treasure, policies, services, programs, professional practices, and love for people will be also. With a clean, well-functioning heart, tomorrow[31] will be a much better place on the other side of now. It has been a long time coming, but a change will come.[32]

---

[31] Tevin Campbell, 1989. "Tomorrow (A Better You, Better Me)."
[32] Sam Cooke, 1964. "A Change Is Gonna Come."

Appendix A
Hyperlinks

Hyperlinks to YouTube videos of songs, audio book, film, and poem

Section	Song, Audio Book, Poem, or Film	Link
1.1	"Inner City Blues" by Marvin Gaye	www.youtube.com/watch?v=57Ykv1D0qEE
1.1	"What's Going On" by Marvin Gaye	www.youtube.com/watch?v=ohz6rvWZXRQ
1.4	"I Can't Breathe" by H.E.R.	www.youtube.com/watch?v=E-1Bf_XWaPE&list=RDE-1Bf_XWaPE&start_radio=1
1.4	"In the Land of the Free" by The Killers	www.youtube.com/watch?v=3AMt9ASeojU
1.4	"Get Up Stand Up" by Bob Marley	www.youtube.com/watch?v=X2W3aG8uizA
1.4	*The Fire Next Time* audio book by James Baldwin	www.youtube.com/watch?v=hi43zpigptI
3.1.1	"Black" by Dave	www.youtube.com/watch?v=pDUPSNdmFew
3.1.2.	"This Is America" by Childish Gambino	https://youtu.be/VYOjWnS4cMY.
4.6.3	"And Still I Rise" by Maya Angelou	www.youtube.com/watch?v=JqOqo50LSZ0
4.6.4	*John Lewis: Good Trouble*	www.johnlewisgoodtrouble.com/
5	"White Man's World" by Jason Isbell	www.youtube.com/watch?v=nu4dupoC7EE
5	"We Shall Be Free" by Garth Brooks	www.youtube.com/watch?v=NAOUwFGXJj0
5	"Never Gonna Break My Faith" by Aretha Franklin	www.youtube.com/watch?v=ZLbHi92YOhE
5	"Glory" by Common and John Legend	www.youtube.com/watch?v=HUZOKvYcx_o
5	"Tomorrow" by Quincy Jones and featuring Tevin Campbell	www.youtube.com/watch?v=axg_BD59wbE
5	"A Change Is Gonna to Come" by Sam Cooke	www.youtube.com/watch?v=wEBlaMOmKV4

Appendix B
Instructional Aids

The following material is offered to assist instructors, trainers, and community leaders in using this Element for discussions in the classroom, the training academy, and the community. These aids consist of a curated list of songs that cross multiple genres of music, as well as a video vignette and related discussion guide.

Songs of Progress

Following are songs that call for progress. They are categorized by genre and serve multiple purposes: opening a class session, framing a discussion, reinforcing a point, and closing a gathering.

R&B / Soul
1. Wake Up Everybody – John Legend and The Roots (featuring Common and Melanie Fiona)
2. Stand Up – Cynthia Erivo
3. Rise Up – Andra Day
4. Glory – Common and John Legend
5. 2020 Riots: How Many Times – Trey Songz
6. I Can't Breathe – H.E.R
7. Inner City Blues (Make Me Wanna Holler) – Marvin Gaye
8. What's Going On – Marvin Gaye

Hip Hop
9. The Bigger Picture – Lil Baby
10. Freedom – Beyoncé featuring Kendrick
11. Stay Woke – Meek Mill (featuring Miguel)
12. White Privilege II – Macklemore and Ryan Lewis
13. Sue Me – Wale
14. Fight the Power – Public Enemy
15. Alright – Kendrick Lamar
16. This Is America – Childish Gambino
17. Black – Dave

Country / Rock / Alternative
18. Land of the Free – The Killers
19. White Man's World – Jason Isbell and the 400 Unit

20. We Shall Be Free – Dylan Miller
21. Mississippi, It's Time – Steve Earle
22. What It Means – Drive-By Truckers
23. Imagine – John Lennon & The Plastic Ono Band

Gospel
24. Strong God – Kirk Franklin
25. Never Gonna Break My Faith – Aretha Franklin (featuring The Boys Choir of Harlem)
26. We Shall Overcome – Mahalia Jackson
27. Oh Freedom! – The Golden Gospel Singers
28. Black Lives Matter – BeBe Winans

Reggae
29. Get Up Stand Up – Bob Marley
30. Black People – Junior Kelly

Blues / Classic Soul
31. Someday We'll All Be Free – Donny Hathaway
32. A Change Is Gonna Come – Sam Cooke

Video Vignette

Here is a link to a perspective-taking video vignette and accompanying discussion guide that emerged from a series of listening and learning exchanges affiliated with the Youth & Blue Engagement Project. This project was under the direction of my lab – the Public Engagement in Governance Looking, Listening & Learning Lab – and supported by the Kettering Foundation, City of Promise, the Charlottesville Police Foundation and the Charlottesville Police Department. These products were cocreated, codesigned, and coproduced by a group of middle and high school teens and two police officers who serve Charlottesville, Virginia. The vignette, titled "A Prelude to an Encounter," allows for a series of what-if scenarios to be used that provide police departments the opportunity to cohost a community forum to share their policies, training curriculum, and related practices with members of the public.

• A Prelude to an Encounter: A Perspective Taking Video Vignette www.cityofpromise.org/youthandblue

Bibliography

Abel, J. R. & Deitz, R. (2011). The role of colleges and universities in building local human capital. *Current Issues in Economics and Finance*, 17(6).

Aberbach, J. & Rockman, B. (2002). Conducting and coding elite interviews. *PS: Political Science and Politics*, 35(4), 673–76.

Addington-Hall, J. M. (2007). Survey research: Methods of data collection, questionnaire design and piloting.In J. M. Addington-Hall, E. Bruera, I. J. Higginson, and S. Payne (eds.), *Research Methods in Palliative Care*. New York: Oxford University Press, 61–82.

Alford, J. & Hughes, O. (2008). Public value pragmatism as the next phase of public management. *American Review of Public Administration*, 38(2), 130–48.

Alonso, J. M., Andrews, R., Clifton, J. & Diaz-Fuentes, D. (2019). Factors influencing citizens' coproduction of environmental outcomes: A multi-level analysis. *Public Management Review*, 21(11), 1620–45.

Alpert, G. P. & Dunham, R. G. (2004). *Understanding Police Use of Force: Officers, Suspects, and Reciprocity*. New York: Cambridge University Press.

Alter, A., Stern, C., Granot, Y. & Balcetis, E. (2016). The "Bad Is Black" effect: Why people believe evildoers have darker skin than do-gooders. *Personality and Social Psychology Bulletin*, 42(12), 1653–65.

Archbold, C. A. (2012). *Policing: A Text/Reader*. Sage: Thousand Oaks, CA.

Arnstein, S. (1969). A ladder of participation. *Journal of the American Institute of Planners*, 35(4), 216–24.

Aronie, J. & Lopez, C. E. (2017). Keeping each other safe: An assessment of the use of peer intervention programs to prevent police officer mistakes and misconduct, using New Orleans' EPIC program as a potential national model. *Police Quarterly*, 20(3), 295–321.

Attard, B. (2015). The president's task force on 21st century policing: Independent oversight and police peer intervention training programs that build trust and bring positive change. *National Association for Civilian Oversight of Law Enforcement*.

Badaracco, L. (1997). *Defining Moments: When Managers Must Choose between Right and Right*. Cambridge, MA: Harvard Business Press.

Baumgartner, F. R., Bell, K., Beyer, L., Boldrin, T., Doyle, L., Govan, L., Halpert, J., Hicks, J., Kyriakoudes, K., Lee, C., Leger, M., McAdon, S., Michalak, S., Murphy, C., Neal, E., O'Malley, O., Payne, E., Sapirstein, A.,

Stanley, S. & Thacker, K. (2021). Intersectional encounters, representative bureaucracy, and the routine traffic stop. *Policy Studies Journal.* https://doi .org/10.1111/psj.12382

Beamer, G. (2002). Elite interviews and state politics research. *State Politics & Policy Quarterly*, 2(1), 86–96.

Benfer, E. A. (2015). Health justice: A framework (and call to action) for the elimination of health inequity and social justice. *American University Law Review*, 65(2), 275–352.

Berlin, I. (1976). The structure of the Free Negro caste in the antebellum United States. *Journal of Social History*, 9(3), 297–318.

Bertrand, M. & Mullainathan S. (2004). Are Emily and Greg more employable than Lakisha and Jamal? A field experiment on labor market discrimination. *The American Economic Review*, 94(4), 991–1012.

Bies, K. (2017). Let the sunshine in: Illuminating the powerful role police unions play in shielding police misconduct. *Stanford Law & Policy Review*, 28(1), 109–49.

Blendon, R. & Young, J. (1998). The public and the war on illicit drugs. *Journal of the American Medical Association*, 279(11), 827–32.

Blessett, B., Dodge, J., Edmond, B., Goerdel, H. T., Gooden, S. T., Headley, A. M., Riccucci, N. M. & Williams, B. N. (2019). Social equity in public administration: A call to action. *Perspectives on Public Management and Governance*, 2(4), 283–99.

Börner, K., Sanyal, S. & Vespignani, A. (2007). Network science. *Annual Review of Information Science and Technology*, 41(1), 537–38.

Bovaird, T. (2005). Public governance: Balancing stakeholder power in a network society. *International Review of Administrative Sciences*, 71(2), 217–28.

Bovaird, T. & Loeffler, E. (2013). We're all in this together: Harnessing user and community coproduction of public outcomes. *Institute of Local Government Studies*. Edgbaston, Birmingham, UK: University of Birmingham, ch 4.

Bradford, B. (2014). Policing and social identity: Procedural justice, inclusion and cooperation between police and public. *Policing and Society*, 24(1), 22–43.

Bradley, P. & MacIntyre, A. (2017). Solving the military moral bystander problem with ethics instruction. In D. Carrick, J. Connelly & D. Wetham (eds.). *Making the Military Moral: Contemporary Challenges and Responses in Military Ethics Education*. London, UK: Routledge, 31–51.

Brandsen, T. & Honingh, M. (2018). Definitions of coproduction and cocreation. In T. Brandsen, T. Steen & B. Verschuere (eds.). *CoProduction and CoCreation*. New York: Routledge, 9–17.

Brandsen, T., Steen, T. & Verschuere, B. (eds.) (2018). *CoProduction and CoCreation: Engaging Citizens in Public Services*. New York: Routledge.

Bringle, R. G., Games, R. & Malloy, E. (1999). *Colleges and Universities as Citizens*. Needham Heights, MA: Allyn and Bacon.

Brooks v. *City of Seattle* (2010). 599 F.3d 1018.

Brown, J. (1991). Defining "reasonable" police conduct: *Graham* v. *Connor* and excessive force during arrest. *UCLA Law Review*, 38, 1257–86.

Bruenig, M. (2014). White high school dropouts have more wealth than black and Hispanic college graduates. *Demos*.

Burns, T. & Stalker, G. M. (2005). Mechanistic and organic systems. *Organizational Behavior*, 2, 214–25.

Card, D. (2005). The causal effect of education on earnings. *Handbook of Labor Economics*, 3(A), 1801–63.

CIVIQS.com. (2017–20). *Black Lives Matter*. https://civiqs.com/results/black_li ves_matter?uncertainty=true&annotations=true&zoomIn=true&trendline=true

Close, B. R. (1997). Toward a resolution of the nondiscrimination/discrimination thesis debate in criminology and criminal justice: Revisiting black criminality and institutional racism. Unpublished dissertation, Tallahassee: Florida State University.

Coates, R. D. (2007). Covert racism in the USA and globally. *Sociology Compass*, 2(1).

Cohn, N. & Quealy, K. (2020). How public opinion has moved on Black Lives Matter. *The New York Times*. www.nytimes.com/interactive/2020/06/10/ upshot/black-lives-matter-attitudes.html

Conklin, J. (2006). *Wicked Problems & Social Complexity*. San Francisco, CA: CogNexus Institute.

Conti, J. A. & O'Neil, M. (2007). Studying power: Qualitative methods and the global elite. *Qualitative Research* 7(1), 63–82.

Creswell, J. W. & Poth, C. N. (2016). *Qualitative Inquiry and Research Design: Choosing among Five Approaches*. Thousand Oaks, CA: Sage.

Davis, J. E. (1998). Cultural capital and the role of historically Black colleges and universities in educational reproduction. *African American Culture and Heritage in Higher Education Research and Practice*, 143–53.

De Choudhury, M., Jhaver, S., Sugar, B. & Weber, I. (2016). Social Media Participation in an Activist Movement for Racial Equality. *Proceedings of the ... International AAAI Conference on Weblogs and Social Media. International AAAI Conference on Weblogs and Social Media*, 92–101.

Denzin, N. K. & Lincoln, Y. S. (2005). Introduction: The discipline and practice of qualitative research. In N. K. Denzin & Y. S. Lincoln (eds.). *The Sage*

Handbook of Qualitative Research. Thousand Oaks, CA: Sage Publications Ltd., 1–32.

Dickens, C. (2007). *A Tale of Two Cities*. London: Penguin.

Dudau, A., Glennon, R. & Verschuere, B. (2019). Following the yellow brick road? (Dis)enchantment with codesign, coproduction and value cocreation in public services. *Public Management Review*, 21(11), 1577–94.

Eze, E. (1997). *Race and the Enlightenment: A Reader*. Malden, MA: Wiley-Blackwell.

Fagan, J., Wilkinson D. L. & Davies, G. (2007). Social contagion of violence. *The Cambridge Handbook of Violent Behavior and Aggression*. New York: Cambridge University Press, 688–723.

Federal Law Enforcement Training Center. (nd). Part IX: Tim Miller podcast on qualified immunity. www.fletc.gov/sites/default/files/PartIXQualifiedImmunity.pdf

Feldman, S. (2020). Americans agree with police reform, but defund the police currently a bridge too far. Ipsos.com. www.ipsos.com/en-us/how-americans-feel-about-police-reform

Follett, M. P. (1998). *New State: Group Organization the Solution of Popular Government*. University Park, PA: Penn State Press.

Fredrickson, G. M. (1981). *White Supremacy: A Comparative Study of American and South African History*. New York: Oxford University Press USA.

Freire, P. (1989). *Education for Critical Consciousness*. New York: Continuum.

Fridell, L. A. (2016). Racial aspects of police shootings: Reducing both bias and counter bias. *Criminology and Public Policy*, 15(2), 481–90.

Gabbidon, S. L. (2010). *Race, Ethnicity, Crime, and Justice: An International Dilemma*. Thousand Oaks, CA: Sage.

Gaines, L. K. & Kappeler, V. E. (2014). *Policing in America*. Waltham, MA: Anderson Publishing.

Getty, R. M., Worrall, J. L. & Morris, R. G. (2016). How far from the tree does the apple fall? Field training officers, their trainees, and allegations of misconduct. *Crime and Delinquency*, 62 (6), 821–39.

Gheduzzi, E., Masella, C., Morelli, N. & Graffigna, G. (2020). The Potential Pitfalls of Coproduction: An Overview on the Codesign of Public Services with and for Family Caregivers Living in Rural and Remote Area. PREPRINT (Version 1) available at Research Square: https://assets.researchsquare.com/files/rs-34600/v3/a491ce11-640b-487e-a1f7-7b525dc4e0b2.pdf

Gilliam, Jr, F., Iyengar, S., Simon, A. & Wright, O. (1996). Crime in black and white: The violent, scary world of local news. *Harvard International Journal of Press/Politics*, 1(3), 6–23.

Goffman, E. (1963). Stigma and social identity. In Tammy L. Anderson (ed.). *Understanding Deviance: Connecting Classical and Contemporary Perspectives*. New York: Routledge, 256–65.

Graham v. *Connor*, (1989) 490 US 386.

Grandage, A., Aliperti, B. & Williams, B. N. (2018). Leveraging the intersection of politics, problem and policy in organizational and social change: An historical analysis of the Detroit, Los Angeles and Atlanta police departments. In J. Ward (ed.). *Policing and Race in America: Economic, Political and Social Dynamics*. Lanham, MD: Lexington Books/Rowan and Littlefield, 55–83.

Green, B., Horel, T. & Papachristos, A. V. (2017). Modeling contagion through social networks to explain and predict gunshot violence in Chicago, 2006 to 2014. *Journal of American Medical Association Internal Medicine*, 177(3), 326–33.

Grönroos, C. (2012). Conceptualising value cocreation: A journey to the 1970s and back to the future. *Journal of Marketing Management*, 28(13–14), 1520–34.

Hadden, S. (2001). *Slave Patrols: Law and Violence in Virginia and the Carolinas*. Cambridge, MA: Harvard University Press.

Harkavy, I. (2006). The role of universities in advancing citizenship and social justice in the 21st century. *Education, Citizenship and Social Justice*, 1(1), 5–37.

Harvey, W. S. (2011). Strategies for conducting elite interviews. *Qualitative Research*, 11(4), 431–41.

Head, B. W. (2008). Wicked problems in public policy. *Public Policy*, 3(2), 101–18.

Headley, A. M. & Wright, J. E. (2019). National Police Reform Commissions: Evidence-based practices or unfulfilled promises? *The Review of Black Political Economy*, 46(4), 277–305.

Hill, R. C. & Levenhagen, M. (1995). Metaphors and mental models: Sensemaking and sensegiving in innovative and entrepreneurial activities. *Journal of Management*, 21(6), 1057–74.

Intravia, J., Thompson, A. & Pickett, J. (2020). Net legitimacy: Internet and social media exposure and attitudes toward the police. *Sociological Spectrum*, 1–23.

Ivan, N. (2020). Why are American public schools still segregated? *Berkeley News*.

Jackson, C. & Newall, M. (2020). Americans overwhelmingly view Floyd killing as part of larger problem. Ipsos.com. www.ipsos.com/en-us/new-polls/abc-coronavirus-poll-wave-11

James, L., James, S. M. & Vila, B. J. (2016). Reverse racism effect: Are cops more hesitant to shoot black than white suspects. *Criminology and Public Policy*, 15(2), 457–80.

Jamieson v. *Shaw*, (1985) 776 F.2d 1048.

Jenkins, D. A., Tichavakunda, A. A. & Coles, J. A. (2020). The second ID: Critical race counterstories of campus police interactions with black men at historically white institutions. *Race Ethnicity and Education*, 1–18.

Johnson v. *Glick*, (1973) 481 F.2d 1028.

Kalunta-Crumpton, A. (2010). *Race, Crime, and Criminal Justice: International Perspectives*. New York: Palgrave Macmillan.

Katz, D. & Kahn, R. L. (1971). Organizations and open-systems theory: A summary. In J. Maurer (ed.). *Readings in Organization Theory: Open-System Approaches*. New York: Random House, 13–19.

Kelling, G. & Moore, M. (1988). From political to reform to community: The evolving strategy of police. *Community Policing: Rhetoric or Reality*.

Kezar, A., (2003). Transformational elite interviews: Principles and problems. *Qualitative inquiry*, 9(3), 395–415.

Klockars, C. B., Ivkovic, S. K. & Haberfeld, M. (2000). The Measurement of Police Integrity. U.S. Department of Justice, Office of Justice Programs, National Institute of Justice.

Knodel, J. (1993). The Design and Analysis of Focus Group Studies: A Practical Approach. In David Morgan (ed.). *Successful Focus Groups: Advancing the State of the Art*. Thousand Oaks, CA: Sage Publications, 35–50.

Krippendorf, K. (1980). *Content Analysis: An Introduction to Its Methodology*. Beverly Hills, CA: Sage.

Krishhna, A. (2020). How did "white" become a metaphor for all things good? *The Conversation*. https://theconversation.com/how-did-white-become -a-metaphor-for-all-things-good-140674

Lewis v. *Downs* (1985), 774 F. 2d 711.

Lipsky, M. (2010). *Street-Level Bureaucracy: Dilemmas of the Individual in Public Services*. New York: Russell Sage Foundation.

Lombroso, C., Gibson, M. & Rafter, N. (2006). *Criminal Man*. Durham, NC: Duke University Press.

Loury, G. (2002). The Anatomy of Racial Inequality. Cambridge, MA: Harvard University Press.

Majavu, M. (2020). The "African gangs" narrative: Associating blackness with criminality and other anti-black racist tropes in Australia. *African and Black Diaspora: An International Journal*, 13(1), 27–39.

Manning, K. (1994). Liberation theology and student affairs. *Journal of College Student Development*, 35, 94–7.

Marshall, G. (2005). The purpose, design and administration of a questionnaire for data collection. *Radiography*, 11(2), 131–36.

Marshall, M. N. (1996). Sampling for qualitative research. *Family Practice*, 13 (6), 522–26.

Marsiglia, F. & Williams, J. (2011). Guest editorial: Behavioral health equity: A call to action for social work education. *Journal of Social Work Education*, 47(3), 385–87.

Mayntz, R. (2003). New challenges to governance theory. In H. Band (ed.). *Governance as a Social and Political Communication*. Manchester, UK: Manchester University Press, 27–40.

Meatto, K. (2019). Still separate, still unequal: Teaching about school segregation and educational inequality. *The New York Times*.

Meier, B. P., Robinson, M. D. & Clore, G. L. (2004). Why good guys wear white: Automatic inferences about stimulus valence based on brightness. *Psychological Science*, 15(2), 82–7.

Milem, J. F., Umbach, P. D. & Liang, C. (2004). Exploring the perpetuation hypothesis: The role of colleges and universities in desegregating society. *Journal of College Student Development*, 45(6), 688–700.

Morin, M. (2020). Americans' perceptions of police drop significantly in one week as protests continue, survey finds. *USA Today*. www.usatoday.com /story/news/politics/2020/06/06/americans-views-police-drop-significantly-amid-protests-survey/3159072001

Morison, Kevin P. (2017). *Hiring for the 21st Century Law Enforcement Officer: Challenges, Opportunities, and Strategies for Success*. Washington, DC: Office of Community Oriented Policing Services.

Morrell, K. & Currie, G. (2015). Impossible jobs or impossible tasks? Client volatility and frontline policing practice in urban riots. *Public Administration Review*, 75(2), 264–275.

Mosher, F. (1982). *Democracy and the Public Service*, 2nd ed. New York: Oxford University Press.

Muhammad, K. G., 2019. *The Condemnation of Blackness: Race, Crime, and the Making of Modern Urban America*. Cambridge, MA: Harvard University Press.

Muharrar, M. (1998). Media blackface: "Racial profiling" in news reporting. Fairness and Accuracy in Reporting. https://fair.org/extra/media-blackface/7

Myrdal, G. (1944). *An American Dilemma: The Negro Problem and Modern Democracy*. New York: Harper & Row.

Nabatchi, T., Sancino, A. & Sicilia, M. (2017). Varieties of participation in public services: The who, when, and what of coproduction. *Public Administration Review*, 77(5), 766–76.

Naderifar, M., Goli, H. & Ghaljaie, F. (2017). Snowball sampling: A purposeful method of sampling in qualitative research. *Strides in Development of Medical Education*, 14(3), 1–6.

National Advisory Commission on Civil Disorders. (1968). Report of the National Advisory Commission on Civil Disorders. www.ncjrs.gov /pdffiles1/Digitization/8073NCJRS.pdf

Nicholson-Crotty, S., Nicholson-Crotty, J. & Fernandez, S. (2017). Will more black cops matter? Officer race and police-involved homicides of black citizens. *Public Administration Review*, 77, 206–216.

O'Dowd, M. F. (2020). Explainer: What is systemic racism and institutional racism? *The Conversation*.

OECD (2009). Current and future public governance challenges. *Government at a Glance 2009*. Paris: OECD Publishing.

Osborne, S. P., Strokosch, K. & Radnor, Z. (2018). Coproduction and the cocreation of value in public services: A perspective from service management 1. In T. Brandsen, T. Steen, and B. Verschuere (eds.). *CoProduction and CoCreation*. New York: Routledge, 18–26.

Oshiro, M. & Valera, P. (2018). Framing physicality and public safety: A study of Michael Brown and Darren Wilson. *Inequality, Crime, and Health among African American Males* (Research in Race and Ethnic Relations). Bingley, UK: Emerald Publishing Limited, 207–28.

Ostrom, E. (1990). *Governing the Commons: The Evolution of Institutions for Collective Action*. New York: Cambridge University Press.

Ouellet, M., Hashimi, S., Gravel, J. & Papachristos, A. V. (2019). Network exposure and excessive use of force: Investigating the social transmission of police misconduct. *Criminology and Public Policy, 18* (3), 675–704.

Papachristos, A. V. (2011). The coming of a networked criminology? Using social network analysis in the study of crime and deviance. *Advances in Criminological Theory*, (17), 101–40.

Park, R. E. & Burgess, E. W. (1924). *Introduction to the Science of Sociology*. Chicago: University of Chicago Press.

Patriotta, G. & Brown, A. D. (2011). Sensemaking, metaphors and performance evaluation. *Scandinavian Journal of Management*, 27(1), 34–43.

Pierson v. *Ray* (1967). 386 US 547.

Pitkin, H. (1967). *The Concept of Representation*. Berkeley, CA: University of California Press.

Plé, L. & Cáceres, R. C. (2010). Not always cocreation: Introducing interactional codestruction of value in service-dominant logic. *Journal of Services Marketing*, 24(6), 430–37.

Potter, G. (nd). The history of policing in the United States. *EKU School of Justice Studies*. https://plsonline.eku.edu/sites/plsonline.eku.edu/files/the-history-of-policing-in-us.pdf

President's Task Force on 21st Century Policing. (2015). Final report of the president's Task Force on 21st Century Policing. https://cops.usdoj.gov/pdf/taskforce/taskforce_finalreport.pdf

Quispe-Torreblanca, E. G. & Stewart, N. (2019). Causal peer effects in police misconduct. *Nature Human Behaviour*, 3, 797–807.

Reichel, P. (1988). Southern slave patrol as a transitional police style. *American Journal of Police*, 7(2), 51–77.

Reuter, E. B. (1927). *The American Race Problem*. Oxford, England: Crowell.

Riccucci, N. M., Van Ryzin, G. G. & Lavena, C. F. (2014). Representative bureaucracy in policing: Does it increase perceived legitimacy? *Journal of Public Administration Research and Theory*, 24(3), 537–51.

Riccucci, N. M., Van Ryzin, G. G. & Jackson, K. (2018). Representative bureaucracy, race, and policing: A survey experiment. *Journal of Public Administration Research and Theory*, 28(4), 506–18.

Roithmayr, D. (2016). The dynamics of excessive force. *University of Chicago Legal Forum*, 10.

Rosenbaum, D. P., Maskaly, J., Lawrence, D. S., Escamilla, J. H., Enciso, G., Christoff, T. E. & Posick, C. (2017). The Police-Community Interaction Survey: Measuring police performance in new ways. *Policing: An International Journal of Police Strategies & Management*.

Rushin, S. (2017). Police union contracts. *Duke Law Journal*, 66(6), 1191–1266.

Saucier v. *Katz* (2001). 533 US 194.

Savitz, L. (1970). The dimensions of police loyalty. *American Behavioral Scientist*, 13(5–6), 693–704.

Schuck, A. M. (2018). Women in policing and the response to rape: Representative bureaucracy and organizational change. *Feminist Criminology*, 13(3), 237–59.

Schwartz, J. (2017). How qualified immunity fails. *Yale Law Journal*, 127(2), 6–76.

Shafer, R. (1982). When does police officer's use of force during arrest become excessive as to constitute violation of constitutional rights, imposing liability under federal Civil Rights Act of 1871, 60 A.L.R. Fed. 204.

Smiley, C. & Fakunle, D. (2016). From "brute" to "thug:" The demonization and criminalization of unarmed black male victims in America. *Journal of Human Behavior in the Social Environment*, 26(3–4), 350–66.

Spradley, J. (1979). *The Ethnographic Interview: The Developmental Research Sequence*. Ann Arbor, MI: Holt, Rinehart and Wilson.

Sunshine, J. & Tyler, T.R. (2003). The role of procedural justice and legitimacy in shaping public support for policing. *Law & Society Review*, 37(3), 513–48.

Thompson, J. (2019). The GI bill should've been race neutral, politicos made sure it wasn't. *Military Times*.

Turner, K. B., Giacopassi, D. & Vandiver, M. (2006). Ignoring the past: Coverage of slavery and slave patrols in criminal justice texts. *Journal of Criminal Justice Education*, 17(1), 181–95.

University of Chicago Law School – Global Human Rights Clinic (2020). Deadly discretion: The failure of police use of force policies to meet fundamental international human rights law and standards. *Global Human Rights Clinic,* 14. https://chicagounbound.uchicago.edu/ihrc/14

US Commission on Civil Rights, Office of Public Affairs. (2018). Police use of force: An examination of modern policing practices. www.usccr.gov/pubs/ 2018/11-15-Police-Force.pdf

Uzochukwu, K. & Thomas, J. C. (2018). Who engages in the coproduction of local public services and why? The case of Atlanta, Georgia. *Public Administration Review*, 78(4), 514–26.

Van Evrie, J. H. (1861). *Negroes and Negro Slavery: The First an Inferior Race; The Latter Its Normal Condition*. Van Evrie, Horton & Company.

Vargo, S. L. & Lusch, R. F. (2006). Service-dominant logic: What it is, what it is not, what it might be. In S. L. Vargo and R. F. Lusch (eds.). *The Service-Dominant Logic of Marketing. Dialog, Debate, and Directions*. Armonk, NY: M. E. Sharpe, 43–56.

Vasilogambros, M. (2020). Training police to step in and prevent another George Floyd. *Stateline: The Pew Charitable Trusts*. www.pewtrusts.org /en/research-and-analysis/blogs/stateline/2020/06/05/training-police-to-step -in-and-prevent-another-george-floyd

Voorberg, W. H., Bekkers, V. J. & Tummers, L. G. (2015). A systematic review of cocreation and coproduction: Embarking on the social innovation journey. *Public Management Review*, 17(9), 1333–57.

Walker, S. & Brown, M. (1995). A pale reflection of reality: The neglect of racial and ethnic minorities in introductory criminal justice textbooks. *Journal of Criminal Justice Education*, 6(1), 61–83.

Ward, G. (2016). Microclimates of racial meaning: Historical racial violence and environmental impacts. *Wisconsin Law Review* (3), 576–626.

Weber, M. (1994). Politics as a vocation. In P. Lassman and R. Spiers (eds.). *Weber: Political Writings*. New York: Cambridge University Press.

Websdale, N. (2001). *Policing the Poor: From Slave Plantation to Public Housing*. Boston, MA: Northeastern University Press.

Weir, K. (2016). Policing in black & white. *Monitor on Psychology*, 47(11). www.apa.org/monitor/2016/12/cover-policing

West, C. (1999). *Restoring Hope: Conversations on the Future of Black America*. Boston, MA: Beacon Press.

White, M. D. & Fradella, H. F. (2016). *Stop and Frisk: The Use and Abuse of a Controversial Policing Tactic*. New York: NYU Press.

Wickersham Commission. (1931). National Commission on Law Observance and enforcement: Report on crime and the foreign born (Report No. 10). Washington, DC: Government Printing Office.

Wilkins, V. M. & Williams, B. N. (2008). Black or blue: Racial profiling and representative bureaucracy. *Public Administration Review*, 68, 654–64.

Wilkins, V. M. & Williams, B. N. (2009). Representing blue: Representative bureaucracy and racial profiling in the Latino community. *Administration & Society*, 40(8), 775–98.

Williams, B. N., Brower, R. S. & Klay, W. E. (2016). Community-centered police professionalism: A template for reflective professionals and learning organisations with implications for the coproduction of public safety and public order. *The Police Journal*, 89(2), 151–73.

Williams, B. N., Christensen, R. K., LePere-Schloop, M. & Silk, P. D. (2015). Appraising the appraisal process: Manager and patrol officer perspectives. *The Police Journal*, 88(3), 231–50.

Williams, B. N., LePere-Schloop, M., Silk, P. D. & Hebdon, A. (2016). The coproduction of campus safety and security: A case study at the University of Georgia. *International Review of Administrative Sciences*, 82(1), 110–30.

Wood, G., Roithmayr, D. & Papachristos, A. V. (2019). The network structure of police misconduct. *Socius: Sociological Research for a Dynamic World*, 5, 1–18.

Working Group of Mayors and Police Chiefs. (2015). Strengthening police-community relations in America's cities: A report of the US conference of mayors' working group of mayors and police chiefs. Washington, DC: US Conference of Mayors. http://legacy.usmayors.org/83rdWinterMeeting/media/012215-report-policing.pdf

Zhao, L. & Papachristos, A. V. (2020). Network position and police who shoot. *The Annals of the American Academy of Political and Social Science*, 687(1), 89–112.

Zuckerman H. (1972). Interviewing an ultra-elite. *The Public Opinion Quarterly*, 36, 159–75.

Brian N. Williams

The wolf shall dwell with the lamb, and the leopard shall lie down with the young goat, and the calf and the lion and the fattened calf together; and a little child shall lead them.

Isaiah 11:6

We live in a world inhabited by people and creatures of all kinds. Young children; communal lambs; secretive and elusive leopards; stubbornly independent goats; strong, overpowering lions; and unassuming, fattened calves. This Element is dedicated to the life and legacy of Marcel Jackson Isaac "Jack" Mincey. Jack, with his foundation of faith, infectious smile, sharp wit, and heart of gold, was and continues to be a problem solver, connector, integrator, and bridgebuilder. Thank you for reflecting light, projecting hope, and inspiring compassionate action during your twelve years on earth. In our humanity, we seek to measure time, outputs, impact, and outcome. Jack is an example where those measures are not quantifiable, calculable, or computable. His legacy is qualitative and immeasurable, yet revealing the substance of things hoped for, the evidence of things unseen. Jack is now one of the heavenly lights. Never to be extinguished, shining brightly, piercing through the darkness, and encouraging the display of our better selves as individuals, communities, institutions, and organizations, as a nation and as a global society.

Carmen J'Mae Williams

To the life and legacy of Breonna Taylor. May this Element spark change in your honor.

Domenick E. Bailey

Mom and Dad, I dedicate this Element to you. Thank you for raising Derrick and me in a household where we prayed for the serenity to accept the things we cannot change, the courage to change the things we cannot accept, and the wisdom to know the difference. It is nothing other than that which has led me to this point of compassion and strength, to be able to take on an issue as momentous as race and policing at this point in history. Thank you for everything! I appreciate your love and wisdom more than you know.

Lana-Michelle Homola

To the children of the next generation: May you grow up with a future brighter than the present. This Element is dedicated to you, as you are the ones who inspired its creation. I pray that you are brave in speaking up and fighting for what you believe in, behave ethically in every situation, and remember to love everyone, always. We are working to make the world a better place for you.

Cambridge Elements $\equiv$

Public and Nonprofit Administration

Andrew Whitford
University of Georgia

Andrew Whitford is Alexander M. Crenshaw Professor of Public Policy in the School of Public and International Affairs at the University of Georgia. His research centers on strategy and innovation in public policy and organization studies.

Robert Christensen
Brigham Young University

Robert Christensen is professor and George Romney Research Fellow in the Marriott School at Brigham Young University. His research focuses on prosocial and antisocial behaviors and attitudes in public and nonprofit organizations.

About the Series

The foundation of this series are cutting-edge contributions on emerging topics and definitive reviews of keystone topics in public and nonprofit administration, especially those that lack longer treatment in textbook or other formats. Among keystone topics of interest for scholars and practitioners of public and nonprofit administration, it covers public management, public budgeting and finance, nonprofit studies, and the interstitial space between the public and nonprofit sectors, along with theoretical and methodological contributions, including quantitative, qualitative, and mixed-methods pieces.

The Public Management Research Association

The Public Management Research Association improves public governance by advancing research on public organizations, strengthening links among interdisciplinary scholars, and furthering professional and academic opportunities in public management.

Cambridge Elements ⁼

Public and Nonprofit Administration

Printed in the United States
by Baker & Taylor Publisher Services

Printed in the United States
by Baker & Taylor Publisher Services